7 THEMES IN MODERN VERSE

Other Poetry from Nelson

7 themes in modern verse

selected and edited by

MAURICE WOLLMAN M.A.
formerly of The Perse School, Cambridge

Nelson

Thomas Nelson and Sons Ltd
Nelson House   Mayfield Road
Walton-on-Thames   Surrey
KT12 5PL   UK

51 York Place
Edinburgh
EH1 3JD   UK

Thomas Nelson (Hong Kong) Ltd
Toppan Building 10/F
22A Westlands Road
Quarry Bay   Hong Kong

Distributed in Australia by

Thomas Nelson Australia
480 La Trobe Street
Melbourne   Victoria 3000
and in Sydney, Brisbane, Adelaide and Perth

© Maurice Wollman 1968
First Published by Harrap Ltd 1968
Reprinted: 1970 (twice); 1971; 1972; 1973; 1975;
          1978; 1979; 1980; 1981; 1982; 1983 (twice)
Fifteenth impression Published by Thomas Nelson and Sons Ltd 1984

ISBN 0-17-444140-1
NPN 9 8 7

Printed in Hong Kong

PREFACE

'A poet is a man who sees life today and tomorrow against the background of life in the past.'

The purpose of this book is to show how various modern poets treat seven general 'themes' that are very much parts of our life today. The first six sections deal with man and the world and their relationship in the past and the present. They tell us how some people live and how others would like to live. Most poets, especially most good poets, have something to say about what conclusions the poet has come to about his life and the life of others. Unless we are recluses—and no poet cuts himself off from his fellows unless and until he has lived among them for some time and realized what life means to himself and to them—our relationship with others and with the world of nature and art and science that surrounds us is our greatest interest and our most essential study. Until we can live with others, we cannot live with ourselves. (Some poets paradoxically say that until one has lived with oneself one cannot live with others!)

Adventure in the past has its counterpart today; the moon is now within our reach, and space is navigable. The age of adventure is always being re-born, though in different circumstances, and the hazards are different today and the problems less romantic.

Home-life provides the poet with many subjects seen from various angles. Poets have always found a fruitful subject in intimate personal relationships: love and marriage and children's attitude to parents and grandparents. Although, as Shakespeare says, 'men are merriest when they are from home,' where is one more natural and at ease than at home?

As we grow up, people and circumstances present ever-changing problems. The poet can tell us how to adapt ourselves, how to react, what we might and should feel. Understanding comes slowly or in a flash—of people, of animals, of the meaning of life and change and death.

Sometimes our lives are lived in the country, sometimes in the town, often in both. Much is old and familiar and what we have grown up with; much is new and does not reveal its true meaning for some time. The poet describes and explains, paints and interprets. Many of the phenomena of modern life are the themes of his poems, and what is not in his poem can be understood from what is in it.

In this age of rapid communication, we must learn to beware as well as to listen. The poet admonishes and warns.

The last section deals with the future, which is difficult and uncertain and problematic. But the poet's prophetic eye 'doth glance from heaven to earth, from earth to heaven', and gives a name and address to 'the forms of things unknown'. For another of the poet's functions and powers is to familiarize us with the strange and the remote.

M.W.

CONTENTS

1. *Work and Leisure*

2. *Travel and Adventure*

8 **CONTENTS**

3. *Personal Relationships*

4. *Coming to Terms with People and Life*

5. *With People and Away from People*

6. *Communication*

7. *'The Age of Anxiety'*

SECTION 1

Work and Leisure

The Game

Follow the crowds to where the turnstiles click.
The terraces fill. *Hoompa*, blares the brassy band.
Saturday afternoon has come to Ninian Park
and, beyond the goalposts, in the Canton Stand
between black spaces, a hundred matches spark.

Waiting, we recall records, legendary scores:
Fred Keenor, Hardy, in a royal blue shirt.
The very names, sad as the old songs, open doors
before our time where someone else was hurt.
Now, like an injured beast, the great crowd roars.

The coin is spun. Here all is simplified
and we are partisan who cheer the Good,
hiss at passing Evil. Was Lucifer offside?
A wing falls down when cherubs howl for blood.
Demons have agents: the Referee is bribed.

The white ball smacked the crossbar. Satan rose
higher than the others in the smoked brown gloom
to sink on grass in a ballet dancer's pose.
Again, it seems, we hear a familiar tune
not quite identifiable. A distant whistle blows.

Memory of faded games, the discarded years;
talk of Aston Villa, Orient, and the Swans.

Half-time, the band played the same military airs
as when The Bluebirds once were champions.
Round touchlines the same cripples in their chairs.

Mephistopheles had his joke. The honest team
dribbles ineffectually, no one can be blamed.
Infernal backs tackle, inside forwards scheme,
and if they foul us need we be ashamed?
Heads up! Oh for a Ted Drake, a Dixie Dean.

'Saved' or else, discontents, we are transferred
long decades back, like Faust must pay that fee.
The Night is early. Great phantoms in us stir
as coloured jerseys hover, move diagonally
on the damp turf, and our eidetic visions blur.

God sign our souls! Because the obscure Staff
of Hell rule this world, jugular fans guessed
the result half-way through the second half
and those who know the score just seem depressed.
Small boys swarm the field for an autograph.

Silent the Stadium. The crowds have all filed out.
Only the pigeons beneath the roofs remain.
The clean programmes are trampled underfoot
and natural the dark, appropriate the rain
whilst, under lamp-posts, threatening newsboys shout.

DANNIE ABSE

All-in Wrestlers

These two great men battling like lovers
Groan and pant in limbs that strangle,
Hold and abandon, clip and part.
Such is their longing for one another.

Each is the other's bitter angel,
Yet for love they wrestle, heart to heart.

They stand as close together
As those two young workmen, one of whom
Removes with the wetted corner of
His crumpled handkerchief a splinter
From his mate's left eye, a dumb
Show of man's concern for man, a silent love.

But then a leg is hooked, an arm once more
Is pressed beyond the limits of desire,
And one upon the other falls, who with a yell
Full of imploring anger beats the floor
With helpless fist, while his enemy, with cruel fire,
Grapples the loser to his breast, and screws him into
   hell.

JAMES KIRKUP

Fishermen

This to be peace, they think beside the river
Being adapted well to expectation
And their wives' mutiny at no achievement,
And yet can sit watching the promises
Escape through weeds and make a trial of biting,
Can lose them, thankful that it is not yet
Time to draw in the line and drain the net.

Learning themselves in this uncertainty
Each hardly cares whether a fish is caught,
For here is privacy, each warns himself,
The fish, inquiries in the river, not
When drawn out promises at all
Being so solid on the bank and still.

Only the boys who live in certainty,
With expectation other than the stream,
Jeer at the patience and draw up their net
Of future frogs, the river vague to them
Until it's emptied. But the old men fill
Their eyes with water, leave the river full.

ELIZABETH JENNINGS

Rythm

They dunno how it is. I smack a ball
right through the goals. But they dunno how the
    words
get muddled in my head, get tired somehow.
I look through the window, see. And there's a wall
I'd kick the ball against, just smack and smack.
Old Jerry he can't play, he don't know how,
not now at any rate. He's too flicking small.
See him in shorts, out in the crazy black.
Rythm, he says, and ryme. See him at back.
He don't know nuthing about Law. He'd fall
flat on his face, just like a big sack,
when you're going down the wing, the wind behind
    you
and crossing into the goalmouth and they're roaring
the whole great crowd. They're up on their feet
    cheering.
The ball's at your feet and there it goes, just crack.
Old Jerry dives—the wrong way. And they're jearing
and I run to the centre and old Bash
jumps up and down, and I feel great, and wearing
my gold and purpel strip, fresh from the wash.

IAIN CRICHTON SMITH

Timothy Winters

Timothy Winters comes to school
With eyes as wide as a football-pool,
Ears like bombs and teeth like splinters:
A blitz of a boy is Timothy Winters.

His belly is white, his neck is dark,
And his hair is an exclamation-mark.
His clothes are enough to scare a crow
And through his britches the blue winds blow.

When teacher talks he won't hear a word
And he shoots down dead the arithmetic-bird,
He licks the patterns off his plate
And he's not even heard of the Welfare State.

Timothy Winters has bloody feet
And he lives in a house on Suez Street,
He sleeps in a sack on the kitchen floor
And they say there aren't boys like him any more.

Old Man Winters likes his beer
And his missus ran off with a bombardier,
Grandma sits in the grate with a gin
And Timothy's dosed with an aspirin.

The Welfare Worker lies awake
But the law's as tricky as a ten-foot snake,
So Timothy Winters drinks his cup
And slowly goes on growing up.

At Morning Prayers the Master helves
For children less fortunate than ourselves,
And the loudest response in the room is when
Timothy Winters roars 'Amen!'

So come one angel, come on ten:
Timothy Winters says 'Amen
Amen amen amen amen.'
Timothy Winters, Lord.

Amen.

CHARLES CAUSLEY

Alex at the Barber's

He is having his hair cut. Towels are tucked
About his chin, his mop scalped jokingly.
The face in the mirror is his own face.

The barber moves and chats among the green
And methylated violet, snipper-snips,
Puts scissors down, puts in a plaited flex,

And like a surgeon with his perfumed hands
Presses the waiting skull and shapes the base.
He likes having his hair cut, and the man

Likes cutting it. The radio drones on.
The eyes in the mirror are his own eyes.
While the next chair receives the Demon Blade,

A dog-leg razor nicks a sideburn here;
As from a sofa there a sheet is whisked
And silver pocketed. The doorbell pings.

The barber, frowning, grips the ragged fringe
And slowly cuts. Upon the speckled sheet
The bits fall down and now his hair is cut.

The neighing trams outside splash through the rain.
The barber tests the spray for heat and rubs
Lemon shampoo into his spiky hair.

Bent with his head above the running bowl,
Eyes squeezed shut, he does not see the water
Gurgle and sway like twisted sweetpaper

Above the waste, but, for a moment, tows
A sleigh of polished silver parrots through
Acres of snow, exclaiming soundlessly.

Then towel round head. Head swung gently up.
Eyes padded. As the barber briskly rubs,
The smile in the mirror is his own smile.

JOHN FULLER

A Schoolboy Hero

Your rapid motion caught the eye
Of one slow-moving, rapt and dull.
The quickness of your hand would ply
Lethally round a nest or hole.

The deftness of your feet! You'd scale
The smoothest birch, the tallest pine,
While I, earth-bound and gross and pale,
To looking up at you resign.

Your answers, too—in class they came
Rattling off your tongue, while I
Considered long, was given the cane
And, ignominiously, would cry.

Yet now I write my learned books
And send verse to smart magazines
While you drink in your local pub
After a day tending machines.

Class, class separated us. I went
To the big school—a wished reprieve.
While with the dunces you remained
Longing impatiently to leave.

We never meet or speak or write.
Yet now and again my slow thoughts tend
To picture you—fair, keen and slight—
My earliest, once my dearest, friend.

PHILIP HOBSBAUM

Birches

When I see birches bend to left and right
Across the lines of straighter darker trees,
I like to think some boy's been swinging them.
But swinging doesn't bend them down to stay
As ice-storms do. Often you must have seen them
Loaded with ice a sunny winter morning
After a rain. They click upon themselves
As the breeze rises, and turn many-coloured
As the stir cracks and crazes their enamel.
Soon the sun's warmth makes them shed crystal shells
Shattering and avalanching on the snow-crust—
Such heaps of broken glass to sweep away
You'd think the inner dome of heaven had fallen.
They are dragged to the withered bracken by the load,
And they seem not to break; though once they are
    bowed
So low for long, they never right themselves:
You may see their trunks arching in the woods
Years afterwards, trailing their leaves on the ground
Like girls on hands and knees that throw their hair
Before them over their heads to dry in the sun.
But I was going to say when Truth broke in

With all her matter-of-fact about the ice-storm
I should prefer to have some boy bend them
As he went out and in to fetch the cows—
Some boy too far from town to learn baseball,
Whose only play was what he found himself,
Summer or winter, and could play alone.
One by one he subdued his father's trees
By riding them down over and over again
Until he took the stiffness out of them,
And not one but hung limp, not one was left
For him to conquer. He learned all there was
To learn about not launching out too soon
And so not carrying the tree away
Clear to the ground. He always kept his poise
To the top branches, climbing carefully
With the same pains you use to fill a cup
Up to the brim, and even above the brim.
Then he flung outward, feet first, with a swish,
Kicking his way down through the air to the ground.
So was I once myself a swinger of birches.
And so I dream of going back to be.
It's when I'm weary of considerations,
And life is too much like a pathless wood
Where your face burns and tickles with the cobwebs
Broken across it, and one eye is weeping
From a twig's having lashed across it open.
I'd like to get away from earth awhile
And then come back to it and begin over.
May no fate wilfully misunderstand me
And half grant what I wish and snatch me away
Not to return. Earth's the right place for love:
I don't know where it's likely to go better.
I'd like to go by climbing a birch tree,
And climb black branches up a snow-white trunk
Toward heaven, till the tree could bear no more,
But dipped its top and set me down again.

That would be good both going and coming back.
One could do worse than be a swinger of birches.

                                        ROBERT FROST

Bell Ringer

Carswell, George, is the name,
Rang the bells here, Wells Cathedral,
Seventy-six deafening years, this brass
On the south wall says so;
The silent memorandum of my fame.
Pulled hard at every festival,
Saw from my loft the seasons pass.
Rang in fog, blossom and harvest time, snow;
Mainly tenor, began in 1810,
When in my cocky 'teens,
Learning from the older men,
What every ringer has to know,
The sequence of the rounds and queens.
Was ready with bob majors at Waterloo,
Parties then in all the hotels,
Bonfires, dancing, and hullabaloo;
A peal of muffled bells
Mourned the mad old king,
But merry grandsire triples for the little Victoria;
We fired the bells for her son's christening,
Making one continuous Gloria.
How many times have I bowed my back
Beneath the broad beams of the tower,
Held the swaying ropes, taut and slack,
At weddings of the county families,
Pale daughters, trembling at the knees,
Puffy knights in velvet and lace,
Dowagers with poodles and pedigrees,
Ringing the sharp changes, hour after hour,

Sprinkling a proud shower of wealth
Over moated swans and market place.
Yet, I do not know what they all came to see,
Those crowds of gawking spectators,
The early closing day they buried me,
Or what they thought the fuss was all about;
The lads up in the tower they drank my health
And, bless them, saw me grandly out
To a long and lively set of Steadman Caters.

LEONARD CLARK

Closed Works

There was a steel rail up from the clay-pit.
The truck, hauled up by a winch on a wire hawser,
Went through the doors at the top of a high tower,
Reaching there, was levelled, was seized by the two
    grinning men
(Grinning and waving to one looking up to them,
    admiring them)
Who, pressing a lever, tilted the truck so that the clay
Tumbled and rumbled down into the tower.
                              Uprighted with a toss,
The empty truck, on a slack windlass, down clattered
    the slope
Jangling bang clattering. O lovely the speed, the
    clanging and ringing and
So to have driven one dancing or ruddy-faced wild
    with excitement
At the sight of the truck under the bridge where I
    stood, whether
(Whether smell of the nettles, the tar, white hawthorn
    in summer;
Or reek of bonfires; allotment smells, men on allot-
    ments in autumn);

Prying between the planks of the bridge at the boom-
    ing and the
                and the slow upward long creep or
Glimpsing the jangling quick clattering
                a downward sweet swoop
Of the truck to the bottom: the bottom where it
    bumped and it rumped
On a beamy, wood-soddy dumbness of buffers, where
    it waited
For the tipping of clay-mud, the clay from the hoppers
(Which men pedal like scooters round rims of the
    clay-pit
Rims round the clay-pit are railed; men loading the
    hoppers on rails—
Then one foot on the plate, the other is scooting till,
    grabbing up speed,
They lifted both feet on the plate of the hoppers, so
    running till thump
At the funnel or chute) and how they would pour
The chugg-cloddy lovely, the downy grey mass into
    the chute
Dumping, and thumping in the underneath truck,
    and then once again
The slow, the upward long creep, wire-hawser
    warblingly tight,
So grumpling under the bridge, and you peer through
    the planks
Of the bridge, and you see it—passing below you—
    the lovely,
The lovely, the loaded, the wire-pulled-up-through
Up-going, big-loaded, steady, thick-loaded
Truck
Up to the tower, where it levelled and stopped, was
    tipped
(By two waiting men, dirty their faces, but waving
    and grinning and fine)

Stumbling and mumbling its clay. Then righted
Clanging
                    rang down truck
To the boof of buffers.
O, those Brick Works!

Today I took my young son to show this vast excite-
    ment and glory.
But I find the brick-works to be now closed.
I attempt to translate a marvellously remembered text
But by necessity find failure.
There is an exhausted hole where the clay was used.
The rails around the rim are uprooted.
There are no hoppers; there is no truck;
(The bridge is insecure and the slope is rotting),
There are no two smiling men;
The tower is empty.
No noise.

Yet: All that was dug down for was built up with?
Or (more simply): Works Closed?

                                    FRANCIS BERRY

The Man in the Bowler Hat

I am the unnoticed, the unnoticeable man:
The man who sat on your right in the morning train:
The man you looked through like a windowpane:
The man who was the colour of the carriage, the colour
    of the mounting
Morning pipe smoke.

I am the man too busy with a living to live,
Too hurried and worried to see and smell and touch:
The man who is patient too long and obeys too much
And wishes too softly and seldom.

I am the man they call the nation's backbone,
Who am boneless—playable catgut, pliable clay:
The Man they label Little lest one day
I dare to grow.

I am the rails on which the moment passes,
The megaphone for many words and voices:
I am graph, diagram,
Composite face.

I am the led, the easily-fed,
The tool, the not-quite-fool,
The would-be-safe-and-sound,
The uncomplaining, bound,
The dust fine-ground,
Stone-for- a-statue waveworn pebble-round.

A. S. J. TESSIMOND

Hobbs

When Hobbs of the piston pace and the bowler hat
And the swinging case is catching his eight-fifteen,
Suburbia's eye at his bobbing by looks pat
To the mantel clock and checks machine with machine.

'I love this walk to the train, and the walk again
At the other end, to my desk and business drive,
Then both in reverse and none the worse for the rain',
Chirps Hobbs as his bowler bobs from the
    half-past-five.

Was he ever a boy who dreamed in hearth-rug joy
Of cities that shone in the fire, or mused on maps
That flickered and whispered of Trebizond and Troy,
And himself let loose? Perhaps, long ago, perhaps.

At least when the morning train is gone, and steam
Thins out from under the bridge, we may surmise,
Some wisp of Hobbs, some otherself of dream
Escapes in archipelagoes of clouds, and sighs.

GEOFFREY JOHNSON

Variations on a Theme

'I spent my youth by a harbour where the sun was
    caught;
There were ships ready for each tide and chance,
And everywhere preparation and talk of a voyage
To something extraordinary beyond.

I spent my old age by a harbour where the sun was
    caught,
Reflecting, "Oh, those young voyagers!
Their curious madness and their certain doom,
For certainly they have not returned". '

'I spent my youth in trade of respectable security,
Almost responsible, respectably advised,
With a pipe-dream of a pension round the corner,
And a time for interminable thought.

I spent my old age in trade of respectable security,
And suddenly came upon my body in the garden
With a panama hat on its head, exclaiming,
"The triumph of sagacious trade!" '

'I spent my youth in studies and with books,
Immersed in ritual, on terms with the devout.
The names of art I knew and rare elation
And casual, appropriate metaphor.

I spent my old age in studies and with books,
Leaving investment to the bank, and tax.
Now I appreciate the deference of waiters
And policies, maturing with benefit.'

                                    PETER CHAMPKIN

SECTION 2

Travel and Adventure

Night of the Scorpion

I remember the night my mother
was stung by a scorpion. Ten hours
of steady rain had driven him
to crawl beneath a sack of rice.
Parting with his poison—flash
of diabolic tail in the dark room—
he risked the rain again.
The peasants came like swarms of flies
and buzzed the Name of God a hundred times
to paralyse the Evil One.
With candles and with lanterns
throwing giant scorpion shadows
on the mud-baked walls
they searched for him: he was not found.
They clicked their tongues.
With every movement that the scorpion made
his poison moved in Mother's blood, they said.
May he sit still, they said.
May the sins of your previous birth
be burned away tonight, they said.
May your suffering decrease
the misfortunes of your next birth, they said.
May the sum of evil
balanced in this unreal world
against the sum of good
become diminished by your pain.

May the poison purify your flesh
of desire, and your spirit of ambition,
they said, and they sat around
on the floor with my mother in the centre,
the peace of understanding on each face.
More candles, more lanterns, more neighbours,
more insects, and the endless rain.
My mother, twisted through and through,
groaning on a mat.
My father, sceptic, rationalist,
trying every curse and blessing,
powder, mixture, herb and hybrid.
He even poured a little paraffin
upon the bitten toe and put a match to it.
I watched the flame feeding on my mother.
I watched the holy man perform his rites
to tame the poison with an incantation.
After twenty hours
it lost its sting.

My mother only said
Thank God the scorpion picked on me
and spared my children.

NISSIM EZEKIEL

Jamaican Bus Ride

The live fowl squatting on the grapefruit and bananas
in the basket of the copper-coloured lady
is gloomy but resigned.
The four very large baskets on the floor
are in everybody's way,
as the conductor points out
loudly, often, but in vain.

Two quadroon dandies are disputing
who is standing on whose feet.

When we stop,
a boy vanishes through the door marked ENTRANCE;
but those entering through the door marked EXIT
are greatly hindered by the fact that when we started
there were twenty standing,
and another ten have somehow inserted themselves
into invisible crannies
between dark sweating body and body.

With an odour of petrol
both excessive and alarming
we hurtle hell-for-leather
between crimson bougainvillea blossom
and scarlet poinsettia
and miraculously do not run over
three goats, seven hens and a donkey
as we pray
that the driver has not fortified himself
at Daisy's Drinking Saloon
with more than four rums:
or by the gods of Jamaica
this day is our last!

                                        A. S. J. TESSIMOND

The Goole Captain

One day as I walked by Crocodile Mansions
I met a young woman, sea-green were her eyes.
And she was loud weeping by the banks of the
    Humber,
O, bitter the sound of her sobs and her sighs.

I asked this young woman why she was sore weeping,
'Pray, tell me,' I said, 'why you grieve by the tide?'
And when I had put my arm tightly around her,
In a voice like a sea bird she sadly replied,

'I was born, sir, at Wetwang, but I left the East
    Riding,
With the cows and the sheep as a girl I would roam,
And if I were back with my father and brothers
I'd ne'er leave again the sweet fields of my home.'

So I led her so gently past Crocodile Mansions,
And I took her so gently by the banks of the Humber,
She gave herself freely, her eyes and her kisses,
And I gave her a gold ring and a necklet of amber.

When we parted at stardown no more was she weeping,
But the very next morning as I sailed out with the tide,
She waved to me gaily as we hove round the headland
And I yearned for her beauty to be by my side.

O, I sailed for a year and a day to the Indies
And I came back to England one green day in spring
But I had forgotten the girl with the green eyes,
The necklet of amber, the little gold ring.

But as I was strolling down the Land of Green
    Ginger
While our ship loaded up with a cargo for Poole,
The people they looked at me strangely and whispered,
'O, beware of the faithless young captain from Goole.'

So I went off at once to Crocodile Mansions
To look for my dear love with sea-green eyes,
But no-one would tell me or answer my questions,
O, bitter my heart then and empty my sighs.

Then I met in 'The Dragon' a drunken old sailor
Who told me he'd seen her with a necklet of amber,
A little gold ring and her eyes green and staring
Floating far out to sea by the banks of the Humber.

And I walked for the last time by Crocodile Man-
    sions,
My heart was so full I shed never a tear
O, I looked at the sea and I looked at the Humber
And in every green wave were the eyes of my dear.

LEONARD CLARK

The Survivors

I never told you this.
He told me about it often:
Seven days in an open boat—burned out,
No time to get food:
Biscuits and water and the unwanted sun,
With only the oars' wing-beats for motion,
Labouring heavily towards land
That existed on a remembered chart,
Never on the horizon
Seven miles from the boat's bow.

After two days song dried on their lips;
After four days speech.
On the fifth cracks began to appear
In the faces' masks; salt scorched them.
They began to think about death,
Each man to himself, feeding it
On what the rest could not conceal.
The sea was as empty as the sky,
A vast disc under a dome
Of the same vastness, perilously blue.

But on the sixth day towards evening
A bird passed. No one slept that night;
The boat had become an ear
Straining for the desired thunder
Of the wrecked waves. It was dawn when it came,
Ominous as the big guns
Of enemy shores. The men cheered it.
From the swell's rise one of them saw the ruins
Of all that sea, where a lean horseman
Rode towards them and with a rope
Galloped them up on to the curt sand.

R. S. THOMAS

The Last Galway Hooker

(The *Ave Maria*, launched in 1922, was the last
hooker to be built in Galway)

Where the Corrib river chops through the Claddagh
To sink in the tide-race its rattling chain
The boatwright's hammer chipped across the water

Ribbing this hooker, while a reckless gun
Shook the limestone quay-wall, after the Treaty
Had brought civil war to this fisherman's town.

That 'tasty' carpenter from Connemara, Cloherty,
Helped by his daughter, had half-planked the hull
In his eightieth year, when at work he died,

And she did the fastening, and caulked her well,
The last boat completed with old Galway lines.
Several seasons at the drift-nets she paid

In those boom-years, working by night in channels
With trammel and spillet and an island crew,
Tea-stew on turf in the pipe-black forecastle,

Songs of disasters wailed on the quay
When the tilt of the water heaves the whole shore.
'She was lucky always the *Ave Maria*',

With her brown barked sails, and her hull black tar,
Her forest of oak ribs and the larchwood planks,
The cavern-smelling hold bulked with costly gear,

Fastest in the race to the gull-marked banks,
What harbour she hived in, there she was queen
And her crew could afford to stand strangers drinks,

Till the buyers failed in nineteen twenty-nine,
When the cheapest of fish could find no market,
Were dumped overboard, the price down to nothing;

Until to her leisure a fisher priest walked
By the hungry dockside, full of her name;
Who made a cash offer, and the owners took it.

Then like a girl given money and a home
With no work but pleasure for her man to perform
She changed into white sails, her hold made room

For hammocks and kettles, the touch and perfume
Of priestly hands. So now she's a yacht
With pitch-pine spars and Italian hemp ropes,

Smooth-running ash-blocks expensively bought
From chandlers in Dublin, two men get jobs
Copper-painting her keel and linseeding her throat,

While at weekends, nephews and nieces in mobs
Go sailing on picnics to the hermit islands,
Come home flushed with health having hooked a few
    dabs.

*   *   *

Munich, submarines, and the war's demands
Of workers to feed invaded that party
Like fumes of the diesel the dope of her sails,

When the Canon went east into limed sheep-lands
From the stone and reed patches of lobstermen
Having sold her to one on Cleggan Quay,

Who was best of the boatsmen from Inishbofin,
She his best buy. He shortened the mast, installed
A new 'Ailsa Craig', made a hold of her cabin,

Poured over the deck thick tar slightly boiled;
Every fortnight he drained the sump in the bilge
'To preserve the timbers'. All she could do, fulfilled.

The sea, good to gamblers, let him indulge
His fear when she rose winding her green shawl
And his pride when she lay calm under his pillage:

And he never married, was this hooker's lover,
Always ill-at-ease in houses or on hills,
Waiting for weather, or mending broken trawls:

Bothered by women no more than by the moon,
Not concerned with money beyond the bare need,
In this boat's bows he sheathed his life's harpoon.

A neap-tide of work, then a spring of liquor
Were the tides that alternately pulled his soul,
Now on a pitching deck with nets to hand-haul,

Then passing Sunday propped against a barrel
Winding among words like a sly helmsman
Till stories gathered around him in a shoal.

She was Latin blessed, holy water shaken
From a small whiskey bottle by a surpliced priest,
Madonnas wafered on every bulkhead,

Oil-grimed by the diesel, and her luck lasted
Those twenty-one years of skill buoyed by prayers,
Strength forged by dread from his drowned ancestors.

She made him money, and again he lost it
In the fisherman's fiction of turning farmer:
The cost of timber and engine spares increased,

Till a phantom hurt him, ribs on a shore,
A hull each tide rattles that will never fish,
Sunk back in the sand, a story finished.

*   *   *

We met here last summer, nineteen fifty-nine,
Far from the missiles, the moon-shots, the money,
And we drank looking out on the island quay,

When his crew were in London drilling a motorway.
Old age had smoothed his barnacled will
And with wild songs he sold me the *Ave Maria*.

Then he was alone, stunned like a widower—
Relics and rowlocks pronging from the wall,
A pot of boiling garments, winter everywhere,

Especially in his bones, watching things fall,
Hooks of three-mile spillets, trammels at the foot
Of the unused double-bed—his mind threaded with all

The marline of his days twined within that boat,
His muscles' own shackles then staying the storm
Which now snap to bits like frayed thread.

So I chose to renew her, to rebuild, to prolong
For a while the spliced yards of yesterday.
Carpenters were enrolled, the ballast and the dung

Of cattle he'd carried lifted from the hold,
The engine removed, and the stale bilge scoured.
De Valera's daughter hoisted the Irish flag

At her freshly adzed mast this Shrove Tuesday,
Stepped while afloat between the tackle of the *Topaz*
And the *St. John*, by Bofin's best boatsmen,

All old as himself. Her ghostly sailmaker,
Her inherited boatwright, her dream-tacking steers-
        man
Picked up the tools of their interrupted work,

And in memory's hands this hooker was restored.
Old men my instructors, and with all new gear
May I handle her well down tomorrow's sea-road.

RICHARD MURPHY

The Mountaineers

Despite the drums we were ready to go.
The natives warned us shaking their spears.
Soon we'd look down on them a mile below
rather as Icarus, so many poets ago,
waved to those shy, forlorn ones, dumb on a thumb-
        nail field.
We started easily but oh the climb was slow.

Above us, the red perilous rocks like our pride
rose higher and higher—broken teeth of the moun-
    tain—
while below the dizzy cliffs, the tipsy angles signified
breathless vertigo and falling possible suicide.
So we climbed on, ropes constricting our hearts
    painfully,
our voices babel yet our journey glorified.

The soul too has altitudes and the great birds fly
over. All the summer long we climbed higher,
crag above crag under a copper sulphate sky,
peak above peak singing of the deserted, shy,
inconsolable ones. Still we climb to the chandelier
    stars
and the more we sing the more we die.

So ascending in that high Sinai of the air,
in space and canyons of the spirit, we lost ourselves
amongst the animals of the mountain—the terrible
    stare
of self meeting itself—and no one would dare
return, descend to that most flat and average world.
Rather, we made a small faith out of a tall despair.

Shakespeare, Milton, Wordsworth, came this way
over the lonely precipice, their faces gold
in the marigold sunset. But they could never stay
under the hurricane tree so climbed to allay
that voice which cried: 'You may never climb again.'
Our faces too are gold but our feet are clay.

We discovered more than footprints in the snow,
more than mountain ghost, more than desolate glory,
yet now, looking down, we see nothing below

except wind, steaming ice, floating mist—and so
silently, sadly, we follow higher the rare songs of
    oxygen.
The more we climb the further we have to go.

DANNIE ABSE

Uncle Cyril

Nobody knew whether from East or West,
Pole or Equator, Uncle Cyril would come,
The eager step and the high-pitched voice in the
    hall,
And the favourite Zulu walking-stick, with its
    handle
Carved to a red baboon. And nobody knew
What season of the year, what day, what hour
Uncle Cyril would come; but when he came,
A wind blew into the house, and nothing was the
    same.

We noticed, when we saw him next to Father,
His clothes were not a part of him. He wore them
As though for a charade. The polished shoes
And camphor-smelling suit were a fancy dress—
You had to think of the skin and bones inside.
For he was a bony man, and the skin all mottled
Yellow and tight; he moved in rapid jerks;
A key, you might have thought, had just wound up the
    works.

We'd leave him how-d'you-doing with the elders,
Then listen, till we heard the click of his feet
Along the nursery landing. He was best
Alone with us, alone to the world's end;
While under a black bow-line the surprise

Of pale blue eyes, that never seemed to settle,
Darted about us like the humming-birds
He threw upon the air with quick and shining words.

The tigers leapt from the Natural History,
And quivered with their black and tawny stripes;
The cobras danced and swayed their wicked hoods,
And on the floor the crocodiles lay grinning.
And yet, with Uncle Cyril there to guard us,
We feared them less than Nurse's bogey-man,
Or the thieving gipsies: Nurse lost all her power
To frighten us with the dark, when Uncle had his hour.

We were away through desert, lake and jungle.
Great suns and moons were over us. We felt
Across the sparkling snow Siberia
Prick icy through our furs; or sweating felt
Brown forest, in a dream, along the Amazon
Break into metal butterflies—then woke
In a white village by the shores of Spain,
And watched on white-capped seas for the English
    coast again.

Back in the nursery, he'd give each one
A present from the lands where we had travelled,
A holy ikon, or a scarlet egg
With a crested cock inside it, or a bracelet
Of tiny thick-set beads. And when we asked
Where we should go tomorrow, he'd reply,
'Tomorrow, children, take a silver spoon,
For we must sup with that Grand Mogul in the
    Moon.'

Tomorrow and tomorrow, and he went,
No one knew where. But what did Aunt Jane say
About a black sheep gathering no moss?

And why did Mother shake her head and sigh
'Poor, dear, unhappy Cyril'? We knew better . . .
At last, when he had dwindled out of sight,
The elders turned away with doubtful looks.
But we drew tufty palms in our dull lesson-books.

GEORGE ROSTREVOR HAMILTON

February Floods, 1953

Those who were far inland
Saw, for a moment, the approaching tempest,
A sudden animal raging across the woods,
Bend each tree as a current sways weeds in water.
The racing beast turned the landscape to a storm track
Till it hit the house, cracked the double windows
And blew the barn door to leave empty hinges.

And this after it had been broken
On the cliffs and high hills that intervened to the
    shore,
This—far inland in a valley soliloquy
Where in stifling summers the stream forgets its
    escape
And almost ceases to talk of a fabled sea.

It was only when the surprising night had gone
That, like flotsam hurled with an eddy to lodge in a
    cleft
Among dry rocks, news of the broken coast
Flooded inland.

The air where birds unconcerned were drifting again
Was alive with hourly messages from the sea:
Roads linked the land for help to the disaster,
Rivers, swollen miles up, led again to the sea.

But the delicate structure of sequence is drowned
   with the land
And these days are in no season; they recall frames
In an uncle's sepia hall—with him in a punt
Poling the main street past submerged shop fronts—
But no lives lost there: recalled more
The fireman's helmet in a mothballed cupboard,
Recalled Southampton burning.

But we inland, watching the buds grow out,
Can think but never know what corn land will be like
Where no green shoot will spring for five more years;
And we inland, intent on our sprouting hedges,
Can think but never hear what sea pastures are like
With the walls down like pebbles and the tides flow-
   ing over the land.
With a fir tree for symbol still to watch in the wind
We have time to collect statistics and erect some
   comfort
From appeals and tin boxes passed from hand to
   hand:
But they have only the sea and the tides returning.

Storing a view before the failure of sunlight
We blow on our fingers and know an East Wind
   coming
Which will snatch the rags of a tramp to reveal a
   shadow,
In our minds, of a king, and there he'll nobly suffer.
Only so, inland or flying over the channel,
Hearing the wind or watching the distant water
We glimpse, for a moment, the fullness of the tide.

JENNY JOSEPH

The Combat

It was not meant for human eyes,
That combat on the shabby patch
Of clods and trampled turf that lies
Somewhere beneath the sodden skies
For eye of toad or adder to catch.

And having seen it I accuse
The crested animal in his pride,
Arrayed in all the royal hues
Which hide the claws he well can use
To tear the heart out of the side.

Body of leopard, eagle's head
And whetted beak, and lion's mane,
And frost-grey hedge of feathers spread
Behind—he seemed of all things bred.
I shall not see his like again.

As for his enemy, there came in
A soft round beast as brown as clay;
All rent and patched his wretched skin;
A battered bag he might have been,
Some old used thing to throw away.

Yet he awaited face to face
The furious beast and the swift attack.
Soon over and done. That was no place
Or time for chivalry or for grace.
The fury had him on his back.

And two small paws like hands flew out
To right and left as the trees stood by
One would have said beyond a doubt

This was the very end of the bout,
But that the creature would not die.

For ere the death-stroke he was gone,
Writhed, whirled, huddled into his den,
Safe somehow there. The fight was done,
And he had lost who had all but won.
But oh his deadly fury then.

A while the place lay blank, forlorn,
Drowsing as in relief from pain.
The cricket chirped, the grating thorn
Stirred, and a little sound was born.
The champions took their posts again.

And all began. The stealthy paw
Slashed out and in. Could nothing save
These rags and tatters from the claw?
Nothing. And yet I never saw
A beast so helpless and so brave.

And now, while the trees stand watching, still
The unequal battle rages there.
The killing beast that cannot kill
Swells and swells in his fury till
You'd almost think it was despair.

EDWIN MUIR

The Enemies

Last night they came across the river and
Entered the city. Women were awake
With lights and food. They entertained the band,
Not asking what the men had come to take
Or what strange tongue they spoke
Or why they came so suddenly through the land.

Now in the morning all the town is filled
With stories of the swift and dark invasion;
The women say that not one stranger told
A reason for his coming. The intrusion
Was not for devastation:
Peace is apparent still on hearth and field.

Yet all the city is a haunted place.
Man meeting man speaks cautiously. Old friends
Close up the candid looks upon their face.
There is no warmth in hands accepting hands;
Each ponders, 'Better hide myself in case
Those strangers have set up their homes in minds
I used to walk in. Better draw the blinds
Even if the strangers haunt in my own house.'

ELIZABETH JENNINGS

The History of the Flood

Bang Bang Bang
Said the nails in the Ark.

It's getting rather dark
Said the nails in the Ark.

For the rain is coming down
Said the nails in the Ark

And you're all like to drown
Said the nails in the Ark.

Dark and black as sin
Said the nails in the Ark.

So won't you all come in
Said the nails in the Ark.

But only two by two
Said the nails in the Ark.

So they came in two by two,
The elephant, the kangaroo,
And the gnu,
And the little tiny shrew.

Then the birds
Flocked in like wingéd words:
Two racket-tailed motmots, two macaws,
Two nuthatches and two
Little bright robins.

And the reptiles: the gila monster, the slow-worm,
The green mamba, the cottonmouth and the
    alligator—
All squirmed in;
And after a very lengthy walk,
Two giant Galapagos tortoises.

And the insects in their hierarchies:
A queen ant, a king ant, a queen wasp, a king wasp,
A queen bee, a king bee,
And all the beetles, bugs, and mosquitoes,
Cascaded in like glittering, murmurous jewels.

But the fish had their wish;
For the rain came down.
People began to drown:
The wicked, the rich—
They gasped out bubbles of pure gold,
Which exhalations
Rose to the constellations.

So for forty days and forty nights
They were on the waste of waters
In those cramped quarters.

It was very dark, damp and lonely.
There was nothing to see, but only
The rain which continued to drop
It did not stop.

So Noah sent forth a Raven. The raven said
  'Kark!
I will not go back to the Ark.'
The raven was footloose,
He fed on the bodies of the rich—
Rich with vitamins and goo.
They had become bloated,
And everywhere they floated.
The raven's heart was black,
He did not come back.
It was not a nice thing to do:
Which is why the raven is a token of wrath,
And creaks like a rusty gate
When he crosses your path; and Fate
Will grant you no luck that day:
The raven is fey:
You were meant to have a scare.
Fortunately in England
The raven is rather rare.

Then Noah sent forth a dove
She did not want to rove.
She longed for her love—
The other turtle dove—
(For her no other dove!)
She brought back a twig from an olive-tree.
There is no more beautiful tree
Anywhere on the earth,
Even when it comes to birth
From six weeks under the sea.

She did not want to rove.
She wanted to take her rest,
And to build herself a nest
All in the olive grove.
She wanted to make love.
She thought that was the best.

The dove was not a rover;
So they knew that the rain was over.
Noah and his wife got out
(They had become rather stout)
And Japhet, Ham, and Shem.
(The same could be said of them.)
They looked up at the sky.
The earth was becoming dry.

Then the animals came ashore—
There were more of them than before:
There were two dogs and a litter of puppies;
There were a tom-cat and two tib-cats
And two litters of kittens—cats
Do not obey regulations;
And, as you might expect,
A quantity of rabbits.

God put a rainbow in the sky.
They wondered what it was for.
There had never been a rainbow before.
The rainbow was a sign;
It looked like a neon sign—
Seven colours arched in the skies:
What should it publicize?
They looked up with wondering eyes.

It advertises Mercy
Said the nails in the Ark.

Mercy Mercy Mercy
Said the nails in the Ark.

Our God is merciful
Said the nails in the Ark.

Merciful and gracious
Bang Bang Bang Bang.

JOHN HEATH-STUBBS

Innocent's Song

Who's that knocking on the window,
Who's that standing at the door,
What are all those presents
Lying on the kitchen floor?

Who is the smiling stranger
With hair as white as gin,
What is he doing with the children
And who could have let him in?

Why has he rubies on his fingers,
A cold, cold crown on his head,
Why, when he caws his carol,
Does the salty snow run red?

Why does he ferry my fireside
As a spider on a thread,
His fingers made of fuses
And his tongue of gingerbread?

Why does the world before him
Melt in a million suns,
Why do his yellow, yearning eyes
Burn like saffron buns?

Watch where he comes walking
Out of the Christmas flame,
Dancing, double-talking:

Herod is his name.

CHARLES CAUSLEY

SECTION 3

Personal Relationships

Soap Suds

This brand of soap has the same smell as once in the
    big
House he visited when he was eight: the walls of the
    bathroom open
To reveal a lawn where a great yellow ball rolls back
    through a hoop
To rest at the head of a mallet held in the hands of
    a child.

And these were the joys of that house: a tower with
    a telescope;
Two great faded globes, one of the earth, one of the
    stars;
A stuffed black dog in the hall; a walled garden with
    bees;
A rabbit warren; a rockery; a vine under glass; the
    sea.

To which he has now returned. The day of course is
    fine
And a grown-up voice cries Play! The mallet slowly
    swings,
Then crack, a great gong booms from the dog-dark
    hall and the ball
Skims forward through the hoop and then through
    the next and then

Through hoops where no hoops were and each
    dissolves in turn
And the grass has grown head-high and an angry
    voice cries Play!
But the ball is lost and the mallet slipped long since
    from the hands
Under the running tap that are not the hands of a child.

                LOUIS MacNEICE

To my Mother

Most near, most dear, most loved and most far,
Under the window where I often found her
Sitting as huge as Asia, seismic with laughter,
Gin and chicken helpless in her Irish hand,
Irresistible as Rabelais, but most tender for
The lame dogs and hurt birds that surround her,—
She is a procession no one can follow after
But be like a little dog following a brass band.

She will not glance up at the bomber, or condescend
To drop her gin and scuttle to a cellar,
But lean on the mahogany table like a mountain
Whom only faith can move, and so I send
O all my faith and all my love to tell her
That she will move from mourning into morning.

                GEORGE BARKER

Follower

My father worked with a horse-plough,
His shoulders globed like a full sail strung
Between the shafts and the furrow.
The horses strained at his clicking tongue.

An expert. He would set the wing
And fit the bright steel-pointed sock.
The sod rolled over without breaking.
At the headrig, with a single pluck

Of reins, the sweating team turned round
And back into the land. His eye
Narrowed and angled at the ground,
Mapping the furrow exactly.

I stumbled in his hob-nailed wake,
Fell sometimes on the polished sod;
Sometimes he rode me on his back
Dipping and rising to his plod.

I wanted to grow up and plough,
To close one eye, stiffen my arm.
All I ever did was follow
In his broad shadow round the farm.

I was a nuisance, tripping, falling,
Yapping always, But today
It is my father who keeps stumbling
Behind me, and will not go away.

SEAMUS HEANEY

The Carpenter

With a jack plane in his hands
My father the carpenter
Massaged the wafering wood,
Making it white and true.

He was skilful with his saws,
Handsaw, bowsaw, hacksaw,

And ripsaw with fishes' teeth
That chewed a plank in a second.

He was fond of silver bits,
The twist and countersink—
And the auger in its pit
Chucking shavings over its shoulder.

I remember my father's hands,
For they were supple and strong
With fingers that were lovers—
Sensuous strokers of wood:

He fondled the oak, the strong-man
·Who holds above his head
A record-breaking lift
Of thick commingled boughs;

And he touched with his finger tips
Dark boards of elm and alder,
Spruce, and cherry for lathes
That turned all days to spring.

My father's hands were tender
Upon my tender head,
But they were massive on massive
Beam for building a house,

And delicate on the box wood
Leaning against the wall
As though placed there in a corner
For a moment and then forgotten,

And expert as they decoded
Archives unlocked by the axe—
The pretty medullary rays
Once jammed with a traffic of food

To a watched and desired tree
That he marked and felled in the winter,
The tracks of tractors smashing
The ground where violets grew,

Then bound in chains and dragged
To the slaughtering circular saw:
A railway dulcimer
Rang the passing bell

Of my father's loved ones,
Though there was no grief in him
Caressing the slim wood, hearing
A robin's piccolo song.

CLIFFORD DYMENT

The Lesson

'Your father's gone,' my bald headmaster said.
His shiny dome and brown tobacco jar
Splintered at once in tears. It wasn't grief.
I cried for knowledge which was bitterer
Than any grief. For there and then I knew
That grief has uses—that a father dead
Could bind the bully's fist a week or two;
And then I cried for shame, then for relief.

I was a month past ten when I learnt this:
I still remember how the noise was stilled
In school-assembly when my grief came in.
Some goldfish in a bowl quietly sculled
Around their shining prison on its shelf.
They were indifferent. All the other eyes
Were turned towards me. Somewhere in myself
Pride, like a goldfish, flashed a sudden fin.

EDWARD LUCIE-SMITH

Digging

Between my finger and my thumb
The squat pen rests; snug as a gun.

Under my window, a clean rasping sound
When the spade sinks into gravelly ground:
My father, digging. I look down

Till his straining rump among the flowerbeds
Bends low, comes up twenty years away
Stooping in rhythm through potato drills
Where he was digging.

The coarse boot nestled on the lug, the shaft
Against the inside knee was levered firmly.
He rooted out tall tops, buried the bright edge deep
To scatter new potatoes that we picked
Loving their cool hardness in our hands.

By God, the old man could handle a spade.
Just like his old man.

My grandfather cut more turf in a day
Than any other man on Toner's bog.
Once I carried him milk in a bottle
Corked sloppily with paper. He straightened up
To drink it, then fell to right away
Nicking and slicing neatly, heaving sods
Over his shoulder, going down and down
For the good turf. Digging.

The cold smell of potato mould, the squelch and slap
Of soggy peat, the curt cuts of an edge
Through living roots awaken in my head.
But I've no spade to follow men like them.

Between my finger and my thumb
The squat pen rests.
I'll dig with it.

SEAMUS HEANEY

In Memory of my Grandfather

similie
*- creaky, — *
knarled
old tree

Swearing about the weather he walked in
like an old tree and sat down;
his beard charred with tobacco, his voice
rough as the bark of his cracked hands.

tree again

Whenever he came it was the wrong time.
Roots spread over the hearth, tripped
whoever tried to move about the room;
the house was cramped with only furniture.

But I was glad of his coming. Only
through him could I breathe in the sun
and smell of fields. His clothes reeked
of the soil and the world outside;

geese and cows were the colour he made them,
he knew the language of birds and brought them
singing out of his beard, alive
to my blankets. He was winter and harvest.

Plums shone in his eyes when he rambled
of orchards. With giant thumbs he'd split
an apple through the core, and juice
flowed from his ripe, uncultured mouth.

Then, hearing the room clock chime,
he walked from my ceiling of farmyards
and returned to his forest of thunder;
the house regained silence and corners.

Slumped there in my summerless season
I longed for his rough hands and words
to break the restrictions of my bed,
to burst like a tree from my four walls.

But there was no chance again of miming
his habits or language. Only now,
years later in a cramped city, can I
be grateful for his influence and love.

EDWARD STOREY

My Grandmother

She kept an antique shop—or it kept her.
Among Apostle spoons and Bristol glass,
The faded silks, the heavy furniture,
She watched her own reflection in the brass
Salvers and silver bowls, as if to prove
Polish was all, there was no need of love.

And I remember how I once refused
To go out with her, since I was afraid.
It was perhaps a wish not to be used
Like antique objects. Though she never said
That she was hurt, I still could feel the guilt
Of that refusal, guessing how she felt.

Later, too frail to keep a shop, she put
All her best things in one long narrow room.
The place smelt old, of things too long kept shut,
The smell of absences where shadows come
That can't be polished. There was nothing then
To give her own reflection back again.

And when she died I felt no grief at all,
Only the guilt of what I once refused.
I walked into her room among the tall
Sideboards and cupboards—things she never used
But needed: and no finger-marks were there,
Only the new dust falling through the air.

ELIZABETH JENNINGS

Warning

When I am an old woman I shall wear purple
With a red hat which doesn't go, and doesn't suit me,
And I shall spend my pension on brandy and summer
  gloves
And satin sandals, and say we've no money for butter.
I shall sit down on the pavement when I'm tired
And gobble up samples in shops and press alarm
  bells
And run my stick along the public railings
And make up for the sobriety of my youth.
I shall go out in my slippers in the rain
And pick the flowers in other people's gardens
And learn to spit.

You can wear terrible shirts and grow more fat
And eat three pounds of sausages at a go
Or only bread and pickle for a week
And hoard pens and pencils and beermats and things
  in boxes.

But now we must have clothes that keep us dry
And pay our rent and not swear in the street
And set a good example for the children.
We will have friends to dinner and read the papers.

But maybe I ought to practise a little now?
So people who know me are not too shocked and
  surprised
When suddenly I am old and start to wear purple.

                                    JENNY JOSEPH

The Smell of Cooking

The smell of cooking rising to my room
Speaks clear of childhood and of many things.
Always, these days, I'm near to tears because
My parents and myself are leaving home.
Even to things that hurt affection clings.

Day after day, I've sorted out my books:
Nothing sensational and yet the whole
Experience is like an open nerve.
My parents and myself exchange cold looks.
Oh, every room is like a brimming bowl

Where flowers are leaning out and wanting air.
We too. The smell of cooking rises high
But hardly touches me because I know
Three-quarters of me is no longer here.

And yet I love this torn, reproachful sky
And am afraid of where I have to go.

                                 ELIZABETH JENNINGS

Symptoms of Love

Love is a universal migraine,
A bright stain on the vision
Blotting out reason.

Symptoms of true love
Are leanness, jealousy,
Laggard dawns;

Are omens and nightmares—
Listening for a knock,
Waiting for a sign:

For a touch of her fingers
In a darkened room,
For a searching look.

Take courage, lover!
Can you endure such grief
At any hand but hers?

ROBERT GRAVES

Twentieth Century Love-song

In these latter days
Few poets have the habit
Of singling out for praise
One woman.

But I am old enough
And of a generation
To vaunt, though crabbed and gruff,
One woman.

Her attributes are such
As most men take for granted,
Until death comes to clutch
One woman.

She is of quiet glance;
But O, her spill of laughter!
All joy is summed by chance
In one woman.

Yet when she hears a tale
Of suffering or evil,
She'll tremble and grow pale,
This woman.

Beyond all laughter's end,
And past the reach of sorrow;
Lover and working friend,
This woman.

But words are too cross-grain
For me to tell the secret
Of what makes her remain
The one woman.

RICHARD CHURCH

The Visitation

Drowsing in my chair of disbelief
I watch the door as it slowly opens—
A trick of the night wind?

Your slender body seems a shaft of moonlight
Against the door as it gently closes.
Do you cast no shadow?

Your whisper is too soft for credence,
Your tread like blossom drifting from a bough,
Your touch even softer.

You wear that sorrowful and tender mask
Which on high mountain tops in heather-flow
Entrances lonely shepherds;

And though a single word scatters all doubts
I quake for wonder at your choice of me:
Why, why and why?

ROBERT GRAVES

The Child Dying

Rhyme
1st & 2nd
4th & 5th
personification
Metaphor
adult perspective on child learning world

Rhyme (
Unfriendly friendly universe,
I pack your stars into my purse,
And bid you, bid you so farewell.
Rhyme (
That I can leave you, quite go out,
Go out, go out beyond all doubt,
My father says, is the miracle.

child going on about the greatness of the Adult.

R (
You are so great, and I so small:
I am nothing, you are all: *Hyperbole*
Being nothing, I can take this way.
R (
Oh I need neither rise nor fall,
For when I do not move at all
I shall be out of all your day.

3rd & 4th fear of death
fear of death and the future

R (
It's said some memory will remain
In the other place, grass in the rain,
Light on the land, sun on the sea,
R (
A flitting grace, a phantom face, *Metaphor*
But the world is out. There is no place
Where it and its ghost can ever be.

personification

R (
Father, father, I dread this air
Blown from the far side of despair,
The cold, cold corner. What house, what hold,

child speaking about death

What hand is there? I look and see
Nothing-filled eternity,
And the great round world grows weak and old. *personification*

Hold my hand, oh hold it fast
I am changing!—until at last
My hand in yours no more will change,
Though yours change on. You here, I there,
So hand in hand, twin-leafed despair—
I did not know death was so strange.

EDWIN MUIR

Death of a Gardener

He rested through the Winter, watched the rain
On his cold garden, slept, awoke to snow
Padding the window, thatching the roof again
With silence. He was grateful for the slow *Metaphor*
Nights and undemanding days; the dark
Protected him; the pause grew big with cold.
Mice in the shed scuffled like leaves; a spark *simile*
Hissed from his pipe as he dreamed beside the fire.

All at once light sharpened; earth drew breath, *Personification*
Stirred; and he woke to strangeness that was Spring,
Stood on the grass, felt movement underneath
Like a child in the womb; hope troubled him to bring
Barrow and spade once more to the waiting soil.
Slower his lift and thrust; a blackbird filled
Long intervals with song; a worm could coil
To safety underneath the hesitant blade.
Hands tremulous as cherry branches kept
Faith with struggling seedlings till the earth
Kept faith with him, claimed him as he slept
Cold in the sun beside his guardian spade.

PHOEBE HESKETH

A Man with a Field

If I close my eyes I can see a man with a load of hay
Cross this garden, guiding his wheelbarrow through
   the copse
To a long, low green-house littered with earthenware,
   glass and clay,
Then prop his scythe near the sycamore to enter it,
   potted with seeds,
And pause where chrysanthemums grow, with
   tomatoes' dragonish beads.
Stooping to fasten the door, he turns on the path
   which leads
To his rain-pitted bedroom of cellos, and low jugs
   catching the drops.

If I open my eyes I see this musician-turned-
   ploughman slow,
Plainly follow his tractor vibrating beneath blue sky,
Or cast his sickle wide, or reach full-length with the hoe,
Or blame the weather that sets its blight on a crop or
   a plan
To mend his roof, or cut back trees where convol-
   vulus ran,
Or attend to as many needs as the holes in a watering-
   can:
He would wait for the better weather; it had been a
   wet July.

This year his field lay fallow; he was late putting
   down his seed.
Cold December concealed with a sighing surplice of
   snow
His waste of neglected furrows, overgrown with
   mutinous weed.

Dark, bereaved like the ground, I found him feeble
   and sick,
And cold, for neither the sticks nor his lamp with a
   shrunken wick
Would light. He was gone through the wicket. His
   clock continued to tick,
But it stopped when the new flakes clustered on an
   empty room below.

                                              VERNON WATKINS

Old Woman

So much she caused she cannot now account for
As she stands watching day return, the cool
Walls of the house moving towards the sun.
She puts some flowers in a vase and thinks
   'There is not much I can arrange
In here and now, but flowers are suppliant

As children never were. And love is now
A flicker of memory, my body is
My own entirely. When I lie at night
I gather nothing now into my arms,
   No child or man, and where I live
Is what remains when men and children go.'

Yet she owns more than residues of lives
That she has marked and altered. See how she
Warns time from too much touching her possessions
By keeping flowers fed, by polishing
   Her fine old silver. Gratefully
She sees her own glance printed on grandchildren.

Drawing the curtains back and opening windows
Every morning now, she feels her years

Grow less and less. Time puts no burden on
Her now she does not need to measure it.
   It is acceptance she arranges
And her own life she places in the vase.

ELIZABETH JENNINGS

Yorkshire Wife's Saga

War was her life, with want and the wild air;
Not for life only; she was out to win.
Houses and ground were cheap, out on the bare
Moor, and the land not bad; they could begin,
Now that the seven sons were mostly men.

Two acres and a sow, on hard-saved brass;
Men down the mine, and mother did the rest.
Pity, with all those sons, they had no lass;
No help, no talk, no mutual interest,
Made fourteen slaving hours empty at best.

Fierce winter mornings, up at three or four;
Men bawl, pigs shriek against the raving beck.
Off go the eight across the mile of moor,
With well-filled dinner-pail and sweat-ragged neck;
But pigs still shriek, and wind blows door off sneck.

Of course they made it; what on earth could stop
People like that? Marrying one by one,
This got a farm, the other got a shop;
Now she was left with but the youngest son,
But she could look about and feel she'd won.

Doctor had told her she was clean worn out.
All pulled to bits, and nowt that he could do.

But plenty get that way, or die, without
Having a ruddy ten-quid note to show.
She'd got seven thriving sons all in a row.

And grandchildren. She liked going by bus
Or train, to stay a bit in those snug homes.
They were her colonies, fair glorious.
'Sit by the fire, ma, till the dinner comes.
Sit by the fire and cuddle little lass.'

RUTH PITTER

Coming to Terms with People and Life

Law, Like Love

Law, say the gardeners, is the sun,
Law is the one
All gardeners obey
To-morrow, yesterday, to-day.

Law is the wisdom of the old
The impotent grandfathers shrilly scold;
The grandchildren put out a treble tongue,
Law is the senses of the young.

Law, says the priest with a priestly look,
Expounding to an unpriestly people,
Law is the words in my priestly book,
Law is my pulpit and my steeple.

Law says the judge as he looks down his nose,
Speaking clearly and most severely,
Law is as I've told you before,
Law is as you know I suppose,
Law is but let me explain it once more,
Law is the Law.

Yet law-abiding scholars write;
Law is neither wrong nor right,
Law is only crimes

Punished by places and by times,
Law is the clothes men wear
Anytime, anywhere,
Law is Good-morning and Good-night.

Others say, Law is our Fate;
Others say, Law is our State;
Others say, others say
Law is no more
Law has gone away.

And always the loud angry crowd
Very angry and very loud
Law is We,
And always the soft idiot softly Me.

If we, dear, know we know no more
Than they about the law,
If I no more than you
Know what we should and should not do
Except that all agree
Gladly or miserably
That the law is
And that all know this,
If therefore thinking it absurd
To identify Law with some other word,
Unlike so many men
I cannot say Law is again,
No more than they can we suppress
The universal wish to guess
Or slip out of our own position
Into an unconcerned condition.
Although I can at least confine
Your vanity and mine
To stating timidly

A timid similarity,
We shall boast anyway:
Like love I say.

Like love we don't know where or why
Like love we can't compel or fly
Like love we often weep
Like love we seldom keep.

                                    W. H. AUDEN

Prayer before Birth

I am not yet born; O hear me.
Let not the bloodsucking bat or the rat or the stoat or
    the club-footed ghoul come near me.

I am not yet born, console me.
I fear that the human race may with tall walls wall me,
    with strong drugs dope me, with wise lies lure me,
    on black racks rack me, in blood-baths roll me.

I am not yet born; provide me
With water to dandle me, grass to grow for me, trees
    to talk to me, sky to sing to me, birds and a white
    light
        in the back of my mind to guide me.

I am not yet born; forgive me
For the sins that in me the world shall commit, my
        words
    when they speak me, my thoughts when they think
        me,
        my treason engendered by traitors beyond me,
            my life when they murder by means of my
            hands, my death when they live me.

I am not yet born; rehearse me
In the parts I must play and the cues I must take when
   old men lecture me, bureaucrats hector me,
      mountains
        frown at me, lovers laugh at me, the white
          waves call me to folly and the desert calls
            me to doom and the beggar refuses
              my gift and my children curse me.

I am not yet born; O hear me,
Let not the man who is beast or who thinks he is God
   come near me.

I am not yet born; O fill me
With strength against those who would freeze my
   humanity, would dragoon me into a lethal automaton,
      would make me a cog in a machine, a thing with
      one face, a thing, and against all those
        who would dissipate my entirety, would
          blow me like thistledown hither and
            thither or hither and thither
              like water held in the
                hands would spill me

Let them not make me a stone and let them not spill me.
Otherwise kill me.

                          LOUIS MacNEICE

Progress

When the armies marched off,
Cursing the criminal stupidity of their leaders,
To fight for the glory and prosperity
Of the motherland,
The leaders
Did their bit

By putting the prices up;
And when the remnants came back,
Cursing the criminal stupidity of their leaders,
Their leaders did what they could for them
By putting the prices up again.
This so reduced
The prosperity of the country
That new leaders were appointed
Whose criminal stupidity was no less
Than the first.

The only consoling thought is
That somewhere along the line
The idea of glory
Was lost sight of.

NORMAN MaCCAIG

An Exchange between the Fingers and the Toes

Fingers

Cramped, you are hardly anything but fidgets.
We, active, differentiate the digits:
Whilst you are merely *little toe* and *big*
(Or, in the nursery, some futile pig)
Through vital use as pincers there has come
Distinction of the *finger* and the *thumb*;
Lacking a knuckle you have sadly missed
Our meaningful translation to a *fist*;
And only by the curling of that joint
Could the firm *index* come to have a point.
You cannot punch or demonstrate or hold
And therefore cannot write or pluck or mould:
Indeed, it seems deficiency in art
Alone would prove you the inferior part.

Toes

Not so, my friends. Our clumsy innocence
And your deft sin is the main difference
Between the body's near extremities.
Please do not think that we intend to please:
Shut in the dark, we once were free like you.
Though you enslaved us, are you not slaves, too?
Our early balance caused your later guilt,
Erect, of finding out how we were built.
Your murders and discoveries compile
A history of the crime of being agile,
And we it is who save you when you fight
Against the odds: you cannot take to flight.
Despite your fabrications and your cunning,
The deepest instinct is expressed in running.

JOHN FULLER

Household Devils

Pipes don't draw, gas-fires pop,
Sinks get choked, chains won't pull,
Milk turns sour in steamy kitchens,
Cigarette-lighters burst into flames—

Possessed by the little household devils
That grimace at me from recalcitrant objects.

Towards human beings I generally exercise
Reasonable forbearance and charity
(Being the way they are):
A sneak has picked my heart from my pocket—
I bring myself to forgive him.

But *they* more frequently and effectively
Trip my heels into mortal sins
Of rage and blasphemy.

Seven in particular sit on the typewriter
Transforming it into a fiendish device
For mangling communication
It gnashes its forty-two teeth.

So I approach it with the understandable
Reluctance of the male spider
Approaching the female spider
To be chewed up in the act of love.

Articles don't get written,
Poems don't get copied;
The grime of sloth settles on my life.

They remind me also if I only traded
(Like practically everyone else)
My soul and my talent for a little gold
I might after all be graciously living
In easier and sleazier circumstances
Among gadgets and gimmicks which actually work.

JOHN HEATH-STUBBS

Disturbances

After the darkness has come
And the distant 'planes catch fire
In the dusk, coming home,
And the tall church spire
No longer stands on the hill
And the streets are quiet except
For a car-door slamming—well,
You might say the houses slept.
An owl calls from a tree.

This is my house and home,
A place where for several years
I've settled, to which I've come
Happily, set my shears
To the hedge which fronts the place,
Had decorators in,
Altered a former face
To a shape I can call my own.
An owl calls from a tree.

Only, sometimes at night
Or running downhill for a train,
I suddenly catch sight
Of a world not named and plain
And without hedges or walls:
A jungle of noises, fears,
No lucid intervals,
No calm exteriors.
An owl calls from a tree.

The place I live in has
A name on the map, a date
For all that is or was.
I avoid hunger and hate:
I have a bed for the night:
The dishes are stacked in the rack:
I remember to switch off the light:
I turn and lie on my back.
An owl calls from a tree.

ANTHONY THWAITE

Someone Looking

I live in a high room. No one
Walking outside can look at me,
Making the privy public. No one
Except a man in a helicopter,
Nothing except a fly or a bird.
Yet a while ago I stared at eyes
Staring at me through the window pane,
Without liking or disliking, casually,
Curiously and very leisurely.
Now the eyes are gone and there's only glass
Through which I look at a traveller's past;
And I sit and wonder: Whose?

CLIFFORD DYMENT

A Birthday Card to my Best Friend

This is the season when a few
   Dry leaves hang on dry wood,
When snow like peanut butter lies
   In streaks along the road,
When toes are etched by cold, and ears
   Throb in the icy air,
And only by induction we
   Know summer will recur.

Stretched out upon his bed your son
   Grows taller all night long.
The carol singers at the door
   Shuffle through their song.
Today's the day that you were born
   (How many years ago?)
They ring the bell: when they were born
   You were as bald as now.

Asleep upon another bed
    Your wife has ceased to grow;
Will bear (except for accidents)
    No further children now.
Cheek and belly sag with age;
    She's pains across her back;
Yet you must love her, since you've hung
    Three children round her neck.

Others will write the books you've planned,
    Will stand for Parliament,
Make speeches, money, symphonies,
    Sculpt, cure, research, invent;
All you can do is tell your wife
    You love her greying hair,
Give sixpence to the carollers,
    And lend your son the car.

                    LAURENCE LERNER

Cage

The canary measures out its prison.
To perch as quick as camera-shutter, perch
Is left for the little hoop where it can swing.
The next thing is the wiry wall, and cling
With tail and twiggy feet. Then back to perch.
Then it fluffs out its throat and sings, content,
As I can judge, born barred.
There follows its tour of the globe, watch till you tire;
Perch, hoop, and wire,
Perch, wire, and hoop.
A minute shows its life, but I watch hard;
Fascinated, who have to write
An account of myself in five hundred words
For a sociological group.

Neat fists of wire clench around caged birds;
Human cages narrow or retreat.
The dead laws of a stiffening State
Shoot up forests of oppressive iron;
The shouting of each military saviour
Bolts bars of iron;
Money, houses, shudder into iron.
Within that fence I am whatever I am.
And I carry my inherited wish to be free,
And my inherited wish to be tied for ever,
As natural to me as my body.
Unlike the bird in the cage, feather to wire,
I lean out some hours,
I lunge to left, I lunge out to right
And hit no bars that way, only mist's pretence;
I cannot estimate my powers.
But, measuring man and bird,
In this respect the likeness stays:
Much of my life will go to exploring my fence.

BERNARD SPENCER

Nino, the Wonder Dog

A dog emerges from the flies
    Balanced upon a ball.
Our entertainment is the fear
    Or hope the dog will fall.

It comes and goes on larger spheres,
    And then walks on and halts
In the centre of the stage and turns
    Two or three somersaults.

The curtains descend upon the act.
    After a proper pause

The dog comes out between them to
   Receive its last applause.

Most mouths are set in pitying smiles,
   Few eyes are free from rheum:
The sensitive are filled with thoughts
   Of death and love and doom.

No doubt behind this ugly dog,
   Frail, fairly small, and white,
Stands some beneficent protector,
   Some life outside the night,

But this is not apparent as
   It goes, in the glare alone,
Through what it must to serve absurd-
   ities beyond its own.

                        ROY FULLER

The Leopards

One of them was licking the bars of its circus-cage
then gazing out sleepily round the tall tent splendid
just here and there with scarlet and brass,
   till the bang of a whip

Brought the animals lolloping onto their chairs (a tail
hung long and twitching, talking its own thoughts.)
   Possibly
the threat was lies, it was not so much
the percussion

Of the whip, but instead some gipsy trick of the tents
won over these golden kittens to rise and beg
and flaunt their white, powder-puff bellies
(though at the report

Of a lash that curls too near, out flutters a paw
like a discharge from a fuse.)
                     Now they were rolling
and cuddling with the bare-chest tamer;
now cowering at the whip-cut.

With humans one judges better; the tamed, the
    untamed.
It is harder with these pretenders—claws in, out,
—finally snaking off low to the ground:
yet there was a likeness, something stayed and haunted
as they bleared and snarled back over their narrow
    shoulders
at that whip banging.

BERNARD SPENCER

Parting from a Cat

Whoever says farewell,
Has, for acquaintance, Death:
Small death, maybe, but still
Of all things dreaded most.
Yesterday I lost
An old, exacting friend
Who for ten years had haunted
My labours like a ghost,
Making my days enchanted
With feline airs and fancies.
Time, no doubt, will send
Some solace; and I know
Memory enchances
The half-companionship
Which is the most that can
Exist between cat and man.
But even so, I mourn

With a miniature grief
That won't relax its grip
Whichever way I turn,
Seeking to forget
My unimportant pet,
And that all life is brief.

RICHARD CHURCH

Predicament

The Local Authority, preparatory to a widening of a
  road,
Instructed its firm under contract to bring down an
  elm.
So next morning a man swings an axe at the bole,
  and a cry
Instantly awakes, weak as a prayer, shrill in despair.
  Startled,
The man lowers his axe, suspended in air, and
  craftily
Then investigates.
                    Tapping with haft and listening,
  he follows
The cry up the main trunk and along a low branch
  and at last
Traces a dismay to its source.

From a hole by the inside of the bough's elbow—a
  wound
From the tree's earlier years and now so nearly
  healed up
That an original ghastly grin, by the growth of new
  tissue,
Had become a little prissy mouth—from thence the
  whiffling

Appeal, or protest, issued.

                 That this was really so
The man confirmed.

                   A sudden swingeing of the axe
Promotes enormous singing vibrations of an agony
Exquisite, wincing highest in pitch as the tree's
    shudder
Subsides to a dull jar.

                 Satisfied, the man
Now saws off the infected branch above the elbow
    and explores
This eloquent ulna.

               Deep in the socket,
Out of that prissy mouth, that pulpy chamber, he
    now prises
An imploring, a fearing, a mis-shapen, a body swollen,
    wing-shrunken
Deplorably deformed bat.

             Weakling of its brood,
    since the departure
Of its siblings and its dam, it had sustained itself
From the drip of overhead leaves, and from the
    mellow collapse
Of this or that insect—insects, which dancing in a
    swarm in the warm
Of the evening, fell
Into the tree's narrowing orifice, into the maw
Of a bat, a predestined celibate, feeding a
    creature
Growing huger as its own defecation
Narrows its condemned cell.

             The man kills it. So
    prevents
A suffocation, a starvation, a crushing to death, a
    suicide
Involuntary, by one who had never been outside.

The man presents it to the Local Authority's museum,
    and it glares
Or smilingly glowers through the glass of the bottle,
    depending
On the spectator's angle of vision.

                              And then the man,
After his killing of the bat, got on with his real task
And brought the tree crashing down.

                                    Yet, as he avers,
And genuinely, Planting he prefers.

                                    FRANCIS BERRY

Street Accident

In the road ahead of me
A quiet commotion I see.
Sickeningly familiar
Is the long withdrawn stretcher
From the whited limousine.
On the ground lies what has been
A carefree adventurer.
Now the *thing* that does not stir,
Sexless, shapeless, living-dead,
Takes the backward path instead,
Relinquishing the personal plan
For this, to be anonymous man
Or woman, invited to the ward
Or the mortuary board.

By the blanket sits like stone
The recent companion,
A figure, bent with head in hand,
A sculpture hard to understand,
So isolated there that grief
Hesitates to bring relief.

No touch is felt, no coaxing word
From the outside world is heard.

Who they were, and who they are,
Each side of this barrier,
No-one in the crowd discovers:
Man and wife, maybe, or lovers,
Or made intimate by chance
Of this lying circumstance,
Wrongly paired, misunderstood
Through false sacrilege of blood.

Speculation does not last.
Facts are finished now: the worst
That could have been, has come and gone.
All of us must stand alone,
We think, and each a Pharisee,
Thank God for our immunity,
Though posing, somewhat sick and wan,
As a good Samaritan.

With irrational guilt at heart
We look again ere we depart,
And shocked by lack of true distress,
Go about our business.
The quiet road is clear again
Save for a handkerchief, and a stain.

RICHARD CHURCH

Death

Death is so common now. Publicity
Diminishes as it multiplies:
Death on the road, death from smoking,
Death in every breath, in every step death.

Yes, the heart fails daily, we so easily
Become disheartened, take time out to discover
Ways of dodging the struggle before it grips us again
In its living, deadly fascination.
Oh the heart fails daily, but only once
Does it fail to pick up again before
It is absolutely and for ever too late.

Too late to mend: the doctors are silent,
Unable to disagree.
They must watch the spring unwind
With their hands in their pockets.
There is nothing for them to do.

But for some death leaves behind
Practical problems which never die
With any death: they are death's children
And we who live their worried guardians.

Only, each time for one, all problems are solved.
It is as if
He who lies dead lies smiling as he thinks
Of the exemption he has won. He has found out
Where it all leads and is telling us
What we have always known but have to be told
Each time, in every death,
So that which is common may put on uncommonness.

And our turn too will come, our turn will come.
There will come the spring at last when spring will
    come no more,
As for him this has not come:
When the spring will come no more and the heart
    no more
Suffer and want things different, for all things

Will be, as for him now they are, out of his folded
  hands
That quietly wait for those who wait
To see it his way too.

Death is so common, but more than ever is only
Real when it becomes a death for you: your death.
Not when you die
(For that is a death for others)
But when someone gives you a death—
Not a newspaper death, an undifferentiated death
At which you can shrug your shoulders and turn to
  another page—
But a death for you to deal with,
A death you have been given and cannot refuse.

That death is yours which will teach you
All that can be learned about death.
And when you die yourself
That will be something for someone else to learn.
The death we know in our life is the only death we
  know,
Our certain share of immortality.

K. W. GRANSDEN

With People and away from People

Loneliness

Nightmare town,
The streets silent, dark;
Sabbath empty
Follow me home:
I walk slowly
And the rain wet stones
Wink under the sodium flares,
I hear them snigger
As I bend my head to the rain:
I must have walked this road
This endless road
A thousand years,
Yet I never meet a soul,
Even the paper scraps
Draw themselves aside,
The houses draw up
From their dank gardens,
But their prim laces never stir—
Oh God is there no one in this town?

MARGARET TAYLOR

Entering the City

The city lies ahead. The vale
is cluttering as the train speeds through.
Hacked woods fall back; the scoop and swell
of cooling towers swing into view.

Acres of clinker, slag-heaps, roads
where lorries rev and tip all night,
railway sidings, broken sheds,
brutally bare in arc-light,

summon me to a present far
from Pericles's Athens, Caesar's Rome,
to follow again the river's scar
squirming beneath detergent foam.

I close the book and rub the glass;
a glance ambiguously dark
entertains briefly scrap-yards, rows
of houses, and a treeless park,

like passing thoughts. Across my head
sundry familiar and strange
denizens of the city tread
vistas I would, and would not, change.

Birth-place and home! The diesels' whine
flattens. Excited and defiled
once more, I heave the window down
and thrust my head out like a child.

TONY CONNOR

Pet Shop

Cold blood or warm, crawling or fluttering
Bric-à-brac, all are here to be bought,
Noisy or silent, python or myna,
Fish with long silk trains like dowagers,
Monkeys lost to thought.

In a small tank tiny enamelled
Green terrapin jostle, in a cage a crowd
Of small birds elbow each other and bicker
While beyond the ferrets, eardrum, eyeball
Find that macaw too loud.

Here behind glass lies a miniature desert,
The sand littered with rumpled gauze
Discarded by snakes like used bandages;
In the next door desert fossilized lizards
Stand in a pose, a pause.

But most of the customers want something comfy—
Rabbit, hamster, potto, puss—
Something to hold on the lap and cuddle
Making believe it will return affection
Like some neutered succubus.

Purr then or chirp, you are here for our pleasure,
Here at the mercy of our whim and purse;
Once there was the wild, now tanks and cages,
But we can offer you a home, a haven,
That might prove even worse.

LOUIS MacNEICE

Valediction for a Branch Railway

The dog-rose in the valley hedge,
Yew and wild cherry on the flinted down
Marked the course of packhorse and of pilgrimage
And the waggoners' tracks to market town,

Dog-rose and yew and cherry too;
High, windy sheep-wolds; fields of moody grain;
Farmhouse orchards; yellow water-meads, and blue
Cabbage acres mark the course of the train.

Steam symbol of an age which meant
Benefits to be lasting; and which lay,
Through the counties or the darkest continent,
A regular solid permanent way.

Join now the legendary charms,
Recalled by place name or by tavern sign.
Soon will *Station Road* or *The Platelayers Arms*
Be the last record of the valley line.

JOHN PUDNEY

Sleeping compartment

I don't like this, being carried sideways
Through the night. I feel wrong and helpless—like
A timber broadside in a fast stream.

Such a way of moving may suit
That odd snake the sidewinder
In Arizona: but not me in Perthshire.

I feel at rightangles to everything,
A crossgrain in existence.—It scrapes
The top of my head, my footsoles.

To forget outside is no help either—
Then I become a blockage
In the long gut of the train.

I try to think I am a through-the-looking-glass
Mountaineer bivouacked
On a ledge five feet high.

It's no good. I go sidelong.
I rock sideways . . . I draw in my feet
To let Aviemore pass.

NORMAN MacCAIG

The Force

At Mrs Tyson's farmhouse, the electricity is pumped
Off her beck-borne wooden wheel outside.
Greased, steady, it spins within
A white torrent, that stretches up the rocks.
At night its force bounds down
And shakes the lighted rooms, shakes the light;
The mountain's force comes towering down to us.

High near its summit the brink is hitched
To an overflowing squally tarn.
It trembles with stored storms
That pulse across the rim to us, as light.

On a gusty day like this the force
Lashes its tail, the sky abounds
With wind-stuffed rinds of cloud that sprout

Clear force, throbbing in squalls off the sea
Where the sun stands poring down at itself
And makes the air grow tall in spurts
Whose crests turn over in the night-wind, foaming.
  We spin
Like a loose wheel, and throbbing shakes our light
Into winter, and torrents dangle. Sun
Pulls up the air in fountains, green shoots, forests
Flinching up at it in spray of branches,
Sends down clear water and the loosened torrent
Down into Mrs Tyson's farmhouse backyard,
That pumps white beams off its crest,
In a stiff breeze lashes its tail down the rocks.

PETER REDGROVE

An Arundel Tomb

Side by side, their faces blurred,
The earl and countess lie in stone,
Their proper habits vaguely shown
As jointed armour, stiffened pleat,
And that faint hint of the absurd—
The little dogs under their feet.

Such plainness of the pre-baroque
Hardly involves the eye, until
It meets his left-hand gauntlet, still
Clasped empty in the other; and
One sees, with a sharp tender shock,
His hand withdrawn, holding her hand.

They would not think to lie so long,
Such faithfulness in effigy
Was just a detail friends would see:

A sculptor's sweet commissioned grace
Thrown off in helping to prolong
The Latin names around the base.

They would not guess how early in
Their supine stationary voyage
The air would change to soundless damage,
Turn the old tenantry away;
How soon succeeding eyes begin
To look, not read. Rigidly they

Persisted, linked, through lengths and breadths
Of time. Snow fell, undated. Light
Each summer thronged the glass. A bright
Litter of birdcalls strewed the same
Bone-riddled ground. And up the paths
The endless altered people came,

Washing at their identity.
Now, helpless in the hollow of
An unarmorial age, a trough
Of smoke in slow suspended skeins
Above their scrap of history,
Only an attitude remains:

Time has transfigured them into
Untruth. The stone fidelity
They hardly meant has come to be
Their final blazon, and to prove
Our almost-instinct almost true:
What will survive of us is love.

PHILIP LARKIN

Wind

This house has been far out at sea all night,
The woods crashing through darkness, the booming
    hills,
Winds stampeding the fields under the window
Floundering black astride and blinding wet

Till day rose; then under an orange sky
The hills had new places, and wind wielded
Blade-light, luminous and emerald,
Flexing like the lens of a mad eye.

At noon I scaled along the house-side as far as
The coal-house door. I dared once to look up—
Through the brunt wind that dented the balls of my
    eyes
The tent of the hills drummed and strained its
    guyrope,

The fields quivering, the skyline a grimace,
At any second to bang and vanish with a flap:
The wind flung a magpie away and a black-
Back gull bent like an iron bar slowly. The house

Rang like some fine green goblet in the note
That any second would shatter it. Now deep
In chairs, in front of the great fire, we grip
Our hearts and cannot entertain book, thought,

Or each other. We watch the fire blazing,
And feel the roots of the house move, but sit on,
Seeing the window tremble to come in,
Hearing the stones cry out under the horizons.

TED HUGHES

At Dunwich

Fifteen churches lie here
Under the North Sea;
Forty-five years ago
The last went down the cliff.
You can see, at low tide,
A mound of masonry
Chewed like a damp bun.

In the village now (if you call
Dunwich a village now,
With a handful of houses, one street,
And a shack for Tizer and tea)
You can ask an old man
To show you the stuff they've found
On the beach when there's been a storm:

Knife-blades, buckles and rings,
Enough coins to fill an old sock,
Badges that men wore
When they'd been on pilgrimage,
Armfuls of broken pots.
People cut bread, paid cash,
Buttoned up against the cold.

Fifteen churches, and men
In thousands working at looms,
And wives brewing up stews
In great grey cooking pots.
I put out a hand and pull
A sherd from the cliff's jaws.
The sand trickles, then falls.

Nettles grow on the cliffs
In clumps as high as a house.
The houses have gone away.
Stand and look at the sea
Eating the land as it walks
Steadily treading the tops
Of fifteen churches' spires.

ANTHONY THWAITE

The Tortoise

Always to be at home
For the tortoise may be as burdensome
As for the human being,
His continuing exile:

The foxes have hide-outs,
The birds of the air their cradles—
They are free to come and go:
To the tortoise, his dome.

'Stroking, a waste of time,'
(Said Sydney Smith) 'You might as well think,
Caressing St Paul's, to please
The dean and Chapter.'

But was wrong,
For he is sensitive,
Even to the roof-tops;
Vegetarian, inoffensive, longaeval,
Condemned, through seven generations
Of men, to trundle
The load of his home-keeping.

JOHN HEATH-STUBBS

The Dam

This was our valley, yes,
Our valley till they came
And chose to build the dam.
All the village worked on it
And we were lucky of course
All through the slump we had
Good jobs; they were too well paid
For the water rose ninety feet,

And covered our houses; yes—
In a midsummer drought
The old church-spire pokes out
And the weather-cock treads the wind
But we were lucky of course
We were—most of us—laid on
Like the water, to the town.
Somehow, I stayed behind.

I work on the Dam, yes—
Do you think the drowned ash-trees
Still have faint impulses
When Spring's up here I wonder?
I was lucky of course
But oh there's a lot of me
Feels like a stifled tree
That went on living, under.

They turn on their taps, yes,
In the dusty city and drink:
Now is it that we sink
Or that the waters rise?
They are lucky of course

But as they go to work
There's an underwater look
In their street-shuttered eyes.

This was our valley, yes,
And I live on the dam
And in my sight the dream
Still drowns the dreamer's home
But I am lucky of course
For in a time of drought
Within me and without
I see where I came from.

PATRIC DICKINSON

Feeding Ducks

One duck stood on my toes.
The others made watery rushes after bread
Thrown by my momentary hand; instead
She stood duck-still and got far more than those.

An invisible drone boomed by
With a beetle in it; the neighbour's yearning bull
Bugled across five fields. And an evening full
Of other evenings quietly began to die.

And my everlasting hand
Dropped on my hypocrite duck her grace of bread.
And I thought, 'The first to be fattened, the first to
  be dead',
Till my gestures enlarged, wide over the darkening
  land.

NORMAN MacCAIG

Cynddylan on a Tractor

Ah, you should see Cynddylan on a tractor.
Gone the old look that yoked him to the soil;
He's a new man now, part of the machine,
His nerves of metal and his blood oil.
The clutch curses, but the gears obey
His least bidding, and lo, he's away
Out of the farmyard, scattering hens.
Riding to work now as a great man should,
He is the knight at arms breaking the fields'
Mirror of silence, emptying the wood
Of foxes and squirrels and bright jays.
The sun comes over the tall trees
Kindling all the hedges, but not for him
Who runs his engine on a different fuel.
And all the birds are singing, bills wide in vain,
As Cynddylan passes proudly up the lane.

R. S. THOMAS

Old Map

Shape of a fat ox,
or mythical beast,
map of my county, 1832.
The paper, handmade, with five
faded tints for roads, rivers,
woodlands, the neighbouring shires;
a sixth colour, the brown stains
dotting the white edges.

Only a few changes, villages
now gone, proud towns
dwindled to villages, commonlands

before they were enclosed,
(I almost hear their larks)
the old words and spellings.

Much that is familiar, Severn
flowing there with same horseshoe bend,
Wye creeping round the western territory,
the great tobacco port, the Cotswold hills,
and my cathedral town.

There to the north a tower marked,
I've said my prayers in its squat church,
those clustering trees are now deep forestlands
where I have wandered at my will,
those fields where now my finger is,
the place where I was born.

LEONARD CLARK

Rookery

Here they come, freckling the sunset,
The slow big sailers bearing down
On the plantation. They have flown
Their sorties and are now well met.

The upper twigs dip and wobble
With each almost two-point landing,
Then ride to rest. There is nothing
Else to do now only settle.

But they keep up a guttural chat
As stragglers knock the roost see-saw.
Something's satisfied in that caw.
Who wouldn't come to rest like that?

SEAMUS HEANEY

Hawk Roosting

I sit in the top of the wood, my eyes closed.
Inaction, no falsifying dream
Between my hooked head and hooked feet:
Or in sleep rehearse perfect kills and eat.

The convenience of the high trees!
The air's buoyancy and the sun's ray
Are of advantage to me;
And the earth's face upward for my inspection.

My feet are locked upon the rough bark.
It took the whole of Creation
To produce my foot, my each feather:
Now I hold Creation in my foot

Or fly up, and revolve it all slowly—
I kill where I please because it is all mine.
There is no sophistry in my body:
My manners are tearing off heads—

The allotment of death.
For the one path of my flight is direct
Through the bones of the living.
No arguments assert my right:

The sun is behind me.
Nothing has changed since I began.
My eye has permitted no change.
I am going to keep things like this.

                                        TED HUGHES

A Road in the Weald

No one would notice that gap between two fields.
Maybe the thought might rise of an irresolute farmer
Who set a hedge, then set a second hedge
Some four yards parallel to it, changing his mind.
Whatever historical conclusions pondering yields,
To pigeon-hole on an archaeological ledge
Of an idly curious brain, there that wasted stretch
Runs to infinity like a rusted road.
It *is* a road: though when the months grow warmer,
The certainty wanes before a river of vetch
That floats a multitudinous traffic of bees
And more ephemeral wings veering between
The encroaching hazels, elders, each with a load
Of music, maybe miniature, but mounting in sum
Through that tunnel of green to a formidable hum,
Yet different from the familiar noise of a road.
Still, this is a road, and has been since, centuries past,
It was laid by a legionary across the vast
And treacherous frontiers so far from home,
Directing another vein to the world's heart—Rome!

RICHARD CHURCH

On the Farm

There was Dai Puw. He was no good,
They put him in the fields to dock swedes,
And took the knife from him, when he came home
At late evening with a grin
Like the slash of a knife on his face.

There was Llew Puw, and he was no good.
Every evening after the ploughing

With the big tractor he would sit in his chair,
And stare into the tangled fire garden,
Opening his slow lips like a snail.

There was Huw Puw, too. What shall I say?
I have heard him whistling in the hedges
On and on, as though winter
Would never again leave those fields,
And all the trees were deformed.

And lastly there was the girl:
Beauty under some spell of the beast.
Her pale face was the lantern
By which they read in life's dark book
The shrill sentence: God is love.

R. S. THOMAS

Granton

A shunting engine butts them
And the long line of waggons
   Abruptly pours out
Iron drops from a bottle.

A flare fizzes, discovers
Tarry sheds, a slipway
   Tasselled with weeds
And a boat with oars akimbo.

On the oily skin of the water
Are coils and whorls, all oily,
   Of green and blue;
They sparkle with filthy coal dust.

Night crouches beyond the harbour,
Powerful, black as a panther
    That suddenly
Opens a yellow eye.

NORMAN MacCAIG

Cornish Cliffs

Those moments, tasted once and never done,
Of long surf breaking in the mid-day sun,
A far-off blow-hole booming like a gun—

The seagulls plane and circle out of sight
Below this thirsty, thrift-encrusted height,
The veined sea-campion buds burst into white

And gorse turns tawny orange, seen beside
Pale drifts of primroses cascading wide
To where the slate falls sheer into the tide.

More than in gardened Surrey, nature spills
A wealth of heather, kidney-vetch and squills
Over these long-defended Cornish hills.

A gun-emplacement of the latest war
Looks older than the hill fort built before
Saxon or Norman headed for the shore.

And in the shadowless, unclouded glare
Deep blue above us fades to whiteness where
A misty sea-line meets the wash of air.

Nut-smell of gorse and honey-smell of ling
Waft out to sea the freshness of the spring
On sunny shallows, green and whispering.

The wideness which the lark-song gives the sky
Shrinks at the clang of sea-birds sailing by
Whose notes are tuned to days when seas are high.

From today's calm, the lane's enclosing green
Leads inland to a usual Cornish scene—
Slate cottages with sycamore between,

Small fields and tellymasts and wires and poles
With, as the everlasting ocean rolls,
Two chapels built for half a hundred souls.

JOHN BETJEMAN

The Condemned

There is a wildness still in England that will not feed
In cages; it shrinks away from the touch of the
     trainer's hand,
Easy to kill, not easy to tame. It will never breed
In a zoo for the public pleasure. It will not be planned.

Do not blame us too much if we that are hedgerow
     folk
Cannot swell the rejoicings at this new world you
     make
—We, hedge-hoggèd as Johnson or Borrow, strange
     to the yoke
As Landor, surly as Cobbett (that badger), birdlike
     as Blake.

A new scent troubles the air—to you, friendly
     perhaps—
But we with animal wisdom have understood that
     smell.

To all our kind its message is Guns, Ferrets, and
    Traps,
And a Ministry gassing the little holes in which we
    dwell.

C. S. LEWIS

Song of the Battery Hen

We can't grumble about accommodation:
we have a new concrete floor that's
always dry, four walls that are
painted white, and a sheet-iron roof
the rain drums on. A fan blows warm air
beneath our feet to disperse the smell
of chicken-shit and, on dull days,
fluorescent lighting sees us.

You can tell me: if you come by
the North door, I am in the twelfth pen
on the left-hand side of the third row
from the floor; and in that pen
I am usually the middle one of three.
But, even without directions, you'd
discover me. I have the same orange-
red comb, yellow beak and auburn
feathers, but as the door opens and you
hear above the electric fan a kind of
one-word wail, I am the one
who sounds loudest in my head.

Listen. Outside this house there's an
orchard with small moss-green apple
trees; beyond that, two fields of
cabbages; then, on the far side of
the road, a broiler house. Listen:

one cockerel grows out of there, as
tall and proud as the first hour of sun.
Sometimes I stop calling with the others
to listen, and wonder if he hears me.

The next time you come here, look for me.
Notice the way I sound inside my head.
God made us all quite differently.
and blessed us with this expensive home.

EDWIN BROCK

SECTION 6

Communication

Anthology

Reading the end-of book biographies
Where those who have done the most say least,
You long for the unofficial truth,
Not sensational, though it might be thought so.

How those two, separate by half an alphabet,
Were lovers. Their poems are half that love.
How this one, hammered by family earning,
Writes duller now than his early daring.

That one's old unrecorded mother
Pivots her life; this one, epileptic,
Has come to humorous terms with existence,
A gentle observer outside the attacks:

All flawed, all unique, only able to speak
Truth in the poem's mouth. Turn back the book.
Print blank pages instead of biographies.
Seek what you look for between their lines.

ROBERT GITTINGS

Communications

With the philosophers in their beleaguered city
(Besieged by warlock words)
Drinking the last dregs
From the central well, until
There is nothing left to drink
(Excepting of course hemlock):

With the scientists shoving their eyebrows
Into the excrement, studying
Animalculae and atoms
Through the wrong end of a micro-telescope
(Besieged by gibbering, non-factual ghosts):

With the poets, writhing as they chew
Their last scrap of toxic laurel
(Besieged by verbal whores,
And the usual poetry-lovers):

With the politicians dreaming of geometry
(Besieged by faceless men)
And the mathematicians dreaming of justice
(Besieged by infinity)—
Each of them wondering whether their separate
    games
Are truly worth the candle:

With the theologians lighting that candle,
Before they collapse at the foot of the altar,
Dumb oxen, stupefied by glory
(Besieged by the single and real
Little Devil of Doubt—'*And you won't
Give me money I'll sweep you all out!*'):

With everyone else, stuck
In front of the blind television set,
Or the radio which breaks down
In the middle of an announcement, merely
That the world is about to come to an end
(Besieged by boredom and commonplace death):

—With these what communication, unless
The courteous angel comes and goes
In diplomatic immunity
With authority to reconstitute a fragmented empire,
Delivering code messages
To which the cipher has been lost:
Conjectured to read 'Love'—
Itself a meaningless word?

JOHN HEATH-STUBBS

Snapshot

Autumn like a pheasant's tail
    lifts over the hedge.

An old man sits in a deckchair
A paperbacked novel on his knees
                            not reading;

His worried wife forks
feebly round her border of michaelmas daisies;
                            not hoping.

Along the lane, a small girl with a pink bow
Runs home looking as contained as an apple;
                            not knowing.

A labourer pushes his bicycle up the hill
Passing beneath the copper pavilion of beech;

                              not seeing.

A poet walks through the village
And like a pickpocket possesses each

                              not belonging.

                              RONALD DUNCAN

Ice on the Round Pond

This was a dog's day, when the land
Lay black and white as a Dalmatian
And kite chased terrier kite
In a Kerry Blue sky.

This was a boy's day, when the wind
Cut tracks in the sky on skates
And noon leaned over like a snowman
To melt in the sun.

This was a poet's day, when the mind
Lay paper-white in a winter's peace
And watched the printed bird-tracks
Turn into words.

                              PAUL DEHN

A New Block

Three hundred fillings high
The functional sandwich soars,
All the silt of an age—
Cars shops offices dingy offices

Luxury flats flatlets
And sour on upper floors
Milk bottles marking the lonely dead.

Three thousand years down
Through how many Troys and Londons
Archaeologists probe; fragments
Of pots and forgotten tongues
Illuminate all. Why
Must we build higher Babels
The less there is to be said?

PATRIC DICKINSON

Behaviour of Money

Money was once well known, like a townhall or the sky
or a river East and West, and you lived one side or
    the other;
Love and Death dealt shocks,
but for all the money that passed, the wise man knew
    his brother.

But money changed. Money came jerking roughly
    alive;
went battering round the town with a boozy, zigzag
    tread.
A clear case for arrest;
and the crowds milled and killed for the pound notes
    that he shed.

And the town changed, and the mean and the little
    lovers of gain
inflated like a dropsy, and gone were the courtesies
that eased the market day;
saying, 'buyer' and 'seller' was saying, 'enemies.'

The poor were shunted nearer to beasts, The cops
  recruited.
The rich became a foreign community. Up there leaped
quiet folk gone nasty,
quite strangely distorted, like a photograph that has
  slipped.

Hearing the drunken roars of Money from down the
  street,
'What's to become of us?' the people in bed would cry:
'And oh, the thought strikes chill;
what's to become of the world if Money should
  suddenly die?

Should suddenly take a toss and go down crack on
  his head?
If the dance suddenly finished, if they stopped the
  runaway bus,
if the trees stopped racing away?
If our hopes come true and he dies, what's to become
  of us?

Shall we recognise each other, crowding around the
  body?
And as we go stealing off in search of the town we
  have known
—what a job for the Sanitary Officials;
the sprawled body of Money, dead, stinking, alone!'

Will X contrive to lose the weasel look in his eyes?
Will the metal go out of the voice of Y? Shall we all
  turn back
to men, like Circe's beasts?
Or die? Or dance in the streets the day that the
  world goes crack?

                                    BERNARD SPENCER

Telephone Conversation

The price seemed reasonable, location
Indifferent. The landlady swore she lived
Off premises. Nothing remained
But self-confession. 'Madam,' I warned,
'I hate a wasted journey—I am African.'
Silence. Silenced transmission of
Pressurized good-breeding. Voice, when it came,
Lipstick coated, long gold-rolled
Cigarette-holder pipped. Caught I was, foully.
'HOW DARK?' . . . I had not misheard. . . . 'ARE YOU
    LIGHT
OR VERY DARK?' Button B. Button A. Stench
Of rancid breath of public hide-and-speak.
Red booth. Red pillar-box. Red double-tiered
Omnibus squelching tar. It *was* real! Shamed
By ill-mannered silence, surrender
Pushed dumbfounded to beg simplification.
Considerate she was, varying the emphasis—
'ARE YOU DARK? OR VERY LIGHT?' Revelation came.
'You mean—like plain or milk chocolate?'
Her assent was clinical, crushing in its light
Impersonality. Rapidly, wave-length adjusted,
I chose. 'West African sepia'—and as afterthought,
'Down in my passport.' Silence for spectroscopic
Flight of fancy, till truthfulness clanged her accent
Hard on the mouthpiece. 'WHAT'S THAT?' conceding

'DON'T KNOW WHAT THAT IS.' 'Like brunette.'
'THAT'S DARK, ISN'T IT?' 'Not altogether.
Facially, I am brunette, but madam, you should see
The rest of me. Palm of my hand, soles of my feet
Are a peroxide blonde. Friction, caused—

Foolishly madam—by sitting down, has turned
My bottom raven black—One moment madam!'—
    sensing
Her receiver rearing on the thunderclap
About my ears—'Madam,' I pleaded, 'wouldn't you
    rather
See for yourself?'

WOLE SOYINKA

Public Bar

A foreign man—God knows,
Malay or Japanese—
Stands in the public bar,
Bracketed off from these
Natives who cannot see
What his credentials are.

Eyes, cheekbones, colour
Of skin, and cut of suit,
And that odd white raincoat—
No one will persecute
This ordinary stranger
For these. But the wrong note

Is struck, all the same.
Simply by being here,
Commenting on the weather,
Drinking a pint of beer,
Having the same again,
All human together,

Won't make him English. 'No,
Everyone has a home.
Though I'm not prejudiced,

No possible good can come
From letting them in.' And so
The foreign man, dismissed

By his normal, human brother,
Stands in the public bar
As if for some offence,
Seeing how things are
With every man a stranger,
Except to indifference.

ANTHONY THWAITE

Baking of Tarts

Today we have Baking of Tarts. Yesterday
We had Simple Salads. And a fortnight tomorrow
We shall have How to Garnish Cod Cutlets. But
    today
Today we have Baking of Tarts. The viewers
Ogle their screens in a flurry of breathless excitement,
For today we have Baking of Tarts.

This is the plastic mixing bowl. And this
Is the rolling-pin and the board, whose use you will
    see
In a moment. And this is the transparent oven
Which in your case you have not got. The speaker
Warms to her theme with ardent, unflagging
    exuberance,
Which in our case we have not got

This is the strawberry jam which is neatly extracted
With a gentle thrust of the spoon. And please do not
    let me
See anyone licking his fingers. It is perfectly easy

If you have any jam in your pot. The viewers
Are silent and motionless, never letting anyone see
Any of them licking their fingers.

And this you can see is the lard. The purpose of this
Is to prevent the pastry from sticking. We can smear
it.
Rapidly backwards and forwards: we call this
Greasing the tin. And rapidly backwards and for-
wards
The viewers are fumbling for biscuits and spilling
their coffee:
They call it ruining the carpet.

They call it ruining the carpet. It is perfectly easy
If your mind is attempting to cope with the cookery
expert
While your hands are engaged in juggling with
saucers and plates
And trying meanwhile to secure a reasonable share
Of the cheese straws, which in our case we have not
got;
For today we have Baking of Tarts.

E. V. MILNER

Attack on the Ad-Man

This trumpeter of nothingness, employed
To keep our reason dull and null and void,
This man of wind and froth and flux will sell
The wares of any who reward him well.
Praising whatever he is paid to praise,
He hunts for ever-newer, smarter ways
To make the gilt seem gold; the shoddy, silk;

To cheat us legally; to bluff and bilk
By methods which no jury can prevent
Because the law's not broken, only bent.

This mind for hire, this mental prostitute
Can tell the half-lie hardest to refute;
Knows how to hide an inconvenient fact
And when to leave a doubtful claim unbacked;
Manipulates the truth but not too much,
And, if his patter needs the Human Touch,
Skilfully artless, artfully naïve,
Wears his convenient heart upon his sleeve.

He uses words that once were strong and fine,
Primal as sun and moon and bread and wine,
True, honourable, honoured, clear and clean,
And leaves them shabby, worn, diminished, mean.
He takes ideas and trains them to engage
In the long little wars big combines wage.
He keeps his logic loose, his feelings flimsy;
Turns eloquence to cant and wit to whimsy;
Trims language till it fits his client's pattern
And style's a glossy tart or limping slattern.

He studies our defences, finds the cracks
And, where the wall is weak or worn, attacks.
He finds the fear that's deep, the wound that's tender,
And, mastered, outmanoeuvred, we surrender.
We who have tried to choose accept his choice
And tired succumb to his untiring voice.
The dripping tap makes even granite soften.
We trust the brand-name we have heard so often
And join the queue of sheep that flock to buy;
We fools who know our folly, you and I.

A. S. J. TESSIMOND

After I wake up

After I wake up and before I get up
I lie in bed each day and think: Supposing,
Only supposing, the leader of some country,
Some party, union, faction, should stand up,
Rise on his hind legs in a public manner,
Get out his sheaf of notes, adjust his glasses,
Sip at his tumbler, hem and haw a little,
Then address his opposition:

Gentlemen,
Gentlemen, we were wrong, we have much wronged
you,
The quarrel was of our seeking and our cause,
We owed you thanks and paid you with resentment,
Some truths we hid and others we perverted,
The abstract words we used were always empty.
Gentlemen,
Gentlemen, we were wrong and with full knowledge
And have no right to count upon forgiveness:
Yet we are human, yet we are both human—
Though you were right, our quarrel grew from
difference
And in that difference lies the birth of richness
As well as of dispute. Let us exchange then,
And build together what we broke together,
Gentlemen,
And live in peace before the eternal darkness.

I dream of that awhile, then sick at heart
Go down to find the newspaper on the mat

HILARY CORKE

SECTION 7

'The Age of Anxiety'

In a Sailplane

Still as a bird
Transfixed in flight
We shiver and flow
Into leagues of light.

Rising and turning
Without a sound
As summer lifts us
Off the ground.

The sky's deep bell
Of glass rings down.
We slip in a sea
That cannot drown.

We kick the wide
Horizon's blues
Like a cluttering hoop
From round our shoes.

This easy 'plane
So quietly speaks,
Like a tree it sighs
In silvery shrieks.

Neatly we soar
Through a roaring cloud:
Its caverns of snow
Are dark and loud.

Into banks of sun
Above the drifts
Of quilted cloud
Our stillness shifts.

Here no curious
Bird comes near.
We float alone
In a snowman's sphere.

Higher than spires
Where breath is rare
We beat the shires
Of racing air.

Up the cliff
Of sheer no-place
We swarm a rope
That swings on space.

Breezed by a star's
Protracted stare
We watch the earth
Drop out of air.

Red stars of light
Burn on the round
Of land: street-constellations
Strew the ground.

Their bridges leap
From town to town:
Into lighted dusk
We circle down.

Still as a bird
Transfixed in flight
We come to nest
In the field of night.

JAMES KIRKUP

At 30,000 feet

A fleck of silver against the darkening blue
The hollow cylinder rockets under the sky's dome,
Unavailingly pursued by the thunder of its sound
Until that final scarlet reverberation;
Like the telegraphed words burning meaninglessly
Upon the slip of yellow paper, and the explosion
Of grief within the mind, this fire and thunder
Do not quite coincide:
The eyes of the watcher see the disaster
Before its voice awakens in his ear.

Nothing that has meaning descends again to earth:
The lighted runway waits vainly
To feel the screeching tyres;
Customs officials will not search this baggage
That downward flakes in dust on silent fields;
Hands cannot clasp, nor lips press
What is now blown weightlessly about the sky.

There was a moment when they drowsed
Deep in luxurious chairs;
Read magazines, wrote letters;

When stewardesses served coffee and liqueurs,
And dirty dishes were neatly stacked
In the bright kitchen.

No other moment followed;
Time stopped. There was nothing . . .

No doubt there is a meaning to this event;
But not the one that can be read
On the white face of the farmer
In mid-furrow gazing upward from his plough,
Nor in the burned minds of those who wait
At the airport barrier.

BERNARD GILHOOLY

To See the Rabbit

We are going to see the rabbit.
We are going to see the rabbit.
Which rabbit, people say?
Which rabbit, ask the children?
Which rabbit?
The only rabbit,
The only rabbit in England,
Sitting behind a barbed-wire fence
Under the floodlights, neon lights,
Sodium lights,
Nibbling grass
On the only patch of grass
In England, in England
(Except the grass by the hoardings
Which doesn't count).
We are going to see the rabbit
And we must be there on time.

First we shall go by escalator,
Then we shall go by underground,
And then we shall go by motorway,
And then by helicopterway,
And the last ten yards we shall have to go
On foot.

And now we are going
All the way to see the rabbit,
We are nearly there,
We are longing to see it,
And so is the crowd
Which is here in thousands
With mounted policemen
And big loudspeakers
And bands and banners,
And everyone has come a long way.
But soon we shall see it
Sitting and nibbling
The blades of grass
On the only patch of grass
In—but something has gone wrong!
Why is everyone so angry,
Why is everyone jostling
And slanging and complaining?

The rabbit has gone,
Yes, the rabbit has gone.
He has actually burrowed down into the earth
And made himself a warren, under the earth,
Despite all these people.
And what shall we do?
What *can* we do?

It is all a pity, you must be disappointed,
Go home and do something else for today,
Go home again, go home for today.
For you cannot hear the rabbit, under the earth,
Remarking rather sadly to himself, by himself,
As he rests in his warren, under the earth:
'It won't be long, they are bound to come,
They are bound to come and find me, even here.'

ALAN BROWNJOHN

The Planster's Vision

Cut down that timber! Bells, too many and strong,
    Pouring their music through the branches bare,
    From moon-white church-towers down the windy air
Have pealed the centuries out with Evensong.
Remove those cottages, a huddled throng!
    Too many babies have been born in there,
    Too many coffins, bumping down the stair,
Carried the old their garden paths along.

I have a Vision of The Future, chum,
    The workers' flats in fields of soya beans
    Tower up like silver pencils, score on score:
And Surging Millions hear the Challenge come
    From microphones in communal canteens
        'No Right! No Wrong! All's perfect, evermore.'

JOHN BETJEMAN

5 Ways to Kill a Man

There are many cumbersome ways to kill a man.
You can make him carry a plank of wood
to the top of a hill and nail him to it. To do this

properly you require a crowd of people
wearing sandals, a cock that crows, a cloak
to dissect, a sponge, some vinegar and one
man to hammer the nails home.

Or you can take a length of steel,
shaped and chased in a traditional way,
and attempt to pierce the metal cage he wears.
But for this you need white horses,
English trees, men with bows and arrows,
at least two flags, a prince and a
castle to hold your banquet in.

Dispensing with nobility, you may, if the wind
allows, blow gas at him. But then you need
a mile of mud sliced through with ditches,
not to mention black boots, bomb craters,
more mud, a plague of rats, a dozen songs
and some round hats made of steel.

In an age of aeroplanes, you may fly
miles above your victim and dispose of him by
pressing one small switch. All you then
require is an ocean to separate you, two
systems of government, a nation's scientists,
several factories, a psychopath and
land that no one needs for several years.

These are, as I began, cumbersome ways
to kill a man. Simpler, direct, and much more neat
is to see that he is living somewhere in the middle
of the twentieth century, and leave him there.

EDWIN BROCK

On Dow Crag

The shepherd on the fell,
With his wild expert cry
Like an atavistic owl,
His dog a vicarious eye

And obedient tentacle,
His rhythm and routine
So nearly animal,
Is yet completely man.

A buzzard rounds its noose
Of hunger high above,
Its eye can split a mouse
If but a whisker move.

—So will it live and die;
No gene within the shell
Shall change its timeless eye
On the shepherd, on the fell,

On the boy who sets the foot
Of the future on Dow Crag,
Who assumes the shepherd's lot,
The buzzard in its egg,

Whose view is incomplete
Till he sees small and far
Like a toy at his feet
Down on the western shore,

The beautiful cooling-towers
Of Calder Hall as strange
As Zimbabwe, as the powers
Of man to suffer change.

PATRIC DICKINSON

Windscale

The toadstool towers infest the shore:
Stink-horns that propagate and spore
    Wherever the wind blows.
Scafell looks down from the bracken band,
And sees hell in a grain of sand,
    And feels the canker itch between his toes.

This is a land where dirt is clean,
And poison pasture, quick and green,
    And storm sky, bright and bare;
Where sewers flow with milk, and meat
Is carved up for the fire to eat,
    And children suffocate in God's fresh air.

NORMAN NICHOLSON

Jodrell Bank

Who were they, what lonely men
Imposed on the fact of night
The fiction of constellations
And made commensurable
The distances between
Themselves, their loves, and their doubt
Of governments and nations?
Who made the dark stable

When the light was not? Now
We receive the blind codes
Of spaces beyond the span
Of our myths, and a long dead star

May only echo how
There are no loves nor gods
Men can invent to explain
How lonely all men are.

PATRIC DICKINSON

Movement of Bodies

Those of you that have got through the rest, I am
    going to rapidly
Devote a little time to showing you, those that can
    master it,
A few ideas about tactics, which must not be confused
With what we call strategy. Tactics is merely
The mechanical movement of bodies, and that is
    what we mean by it.
    Or perhaps I should say: by them.

Strategy, to be quite frank, you will have no hand in.
It is done by those up above, and it merely refers to
The larger movements over which we have no control.
But tactics are also important, together or single.
You must never forget that suddenly, in an engage-
    ment,
    You may find yourself alone.

This brown clay model is a characteristic terrain
Of a simple and typical kind. Its general character
Should be taken in at a glance, and its general
    character
You can see at a glance it is somewhat hilly by nature,
With a fair amount of typical vegetation
    Disposed at certain parts.

Here at the top of the tray, which we might call the
    northwards,
Is a wooded headland, with a crown of bushy-topped
    trees on;
And proceeding downwards or south we take in at a
    glance
A variety of gorges and knolls and plateaus and basins
    and saddles,
Somewhat symmetrically put, for easy identification.
    And here is our point of attack.

But remember of course it will not be a tray you will
    fight on,
Nor always by daylight. After a hot day, think of the
    night
Cooling the desert down, and you still moving over it:
Past a ruined tank or a gun, perhaps, or a dead friend,
Lying about somewhere; it might quite well be that.
    It isn't always a tray.

And even this tray is different to what I had thought.
These models are somehow never always the same;
    the reason
I do not know how to explain quite. Just as I do not
    know
Why there is always someone at this particular lesson
Who always starts crying. Now will you kindly
    Empty those blinking eyes?

I thank you. I have no wish to seem impatient.
I know it is all very hard, but you would not like,
To take a simple example, to take for example,
This place we have thought of here, you would not like
To find yourself face to face with it, and you not
    knowing
    What there might be inside?

Very well then: suppose this is what you must capture.
It will not be easy, not being very exposed,
Secluded away like it is, and somewhat protected
By a typical formation of what appear to be bushes,
So that you cannot see, as to what is concealed inside,
    As to whether it is friend or foe.

And so, a strong feint will be necessary in this
        connection.
It will not be a tray, remember. It may be a desert
        stretch
With nothing in sight, to speak of. I have no wish to
        be inconsiderate,
But I see there are two of you now, commencing to
        snivel.
I cannot think where such emotional privates can
        come from.
    Try to behave like men.

I thank you. I was saying: a thoughtful deception
Is always somewhat essential in such a case. You can
        see
That if only the attacker can capture such an em-
        placement
The rest of the terrain is his: a key-position, and
        calling
For the most resourceful manoeuvres. But that is
        what tactics is.
    Or I should say rather: are.

Let us begin then and appreciate the situation.
I am thinking especially of the point we have been
        considering,
Though in a sense everything in the whole of the
        terrain

Must be appreciated. I do not know what I have said
To upset so many of you. I know it is a difficult
    lesson.
    Yesterday a man was sick,

But I have never known as many as *five* in a single
    intake,
Unable to cope with this lesson. I think you had better
Fall out, all five, and sit at the back of the room,
Being careful not to talk. The rest will close up.
Perhaps it was me saying 'a dead friend', earlier on?
    Well, some of us live.

And I never know why, whenever we get to tactics,
Men either laugh or cry, though neither being strictly
    called for.
But perhaps I have started too early with a difficult
    problem
We will start again, further north, with a simpler
    assault.
Are you ready? Is everyone paying attention?
    Very well then. Here are two hills.

HENRY REED

A Modern Hero

I make arrangements in the house.
I move a vase from here to there.
I use, to keep my light tools neat,
The cupboard by the stair.

I go one distance every day.
I hang my coat upon one peg.
I see my panel doctor when
The vein hurts in my leg.

I work to Tuesday, first of month;
I make my figures up till then.
I carry to the luncheon room
The Telegraph. Ah, when

The known worlds split apart again,
When oceans hurtle from their bed,
Who will see what I have done
Or know what I have said?

PETER CHAMPKIN

Pompeii

What did they do at Pompeii? Go away?
Well, they could go: the world was wide enough,
Three miles would clear them, anywhere would do,
There were other towns and farms in Italy.
Under a fat vineyard something heaved—
High time to pack and scarper? The volcano
However was always there, making particular
Rumblings the less cogent, In the atrium
The new fresco of cupids by Pidonius
Was much admired and would be hard to leave:
Four cows were heavy in calf: the soil besides
Was hugely fertile, sulphur in the tilth,
The grapes grew there like grapefruit. Even when
The earth shook almost open and the cone
Sprouted in giant feathers, it was not
Too late: but let us see what Polpius does,
Whose brother's of the guild of geologues . . .
Running, loving, crouching by pots of gold,
Poor souls, the fire preserved you where you lay;
At which we stare and poke in the museum today.

Our case is somewhat different though not quite—
No matter if history points an altered gun:
Burning by fire or fire will all be one;
Dying in any hour is fall of night.
How constant the rumblings are, yet what's to be
    done
But till our vineyards, paint our atria,
Pay formal visits to the homes of friends,
Love and beget and do what we should do,
Now the whole world is one volcano grown;
And though we would fly, there is nowhere to fly to?

HILARY CORKE

H-Bomb

'If they roosh on like this they'll ruin all,'
Said my old uncle resting on his spade.
'Now in that other war, when you was small,
I dare say you remember how they sprayed
(One summer night), or chance you didn't wake,
Our cricket-ground with bombs—big holes they
    make.

'And them there bombs, six of them in a line,
Lifted the glass out of our blessèd church;
The old East Window went,—the new one's fine
But nought to that: where Jesus used to perch
On that plump donkey bound for Egypt, yes,
That was a work of art,—the donk no less.

'But they're blown up, and Wise Men blown up
    too,—
And what's the score?' I answered. 'Hutton's in!
He's going well.' My uncle: 'Good for you.

What about Hobbs?' 'Hobbs?' 'Where have you
   a-bin?'
Still he forgave me, and allowed me this:
'You've come in a thin time, my little Ciss.'

And then,—'If they go on they'll upset all,
They and their funny bomb. They nearly did
The last time. Up to then I bowled a ball
That came back quick; but where that bomb-hole hid
It never did again. Things aren't the same.
I tell you, girl, they've no sense of a game.'
I watched the old man, and I held my tongue.
He was so simple, and I was so young.

EDMUND BLUNDEN

Science-fiction Cradlesong

By and by Man will try
To get out into the sky,
Sailing far beyond the air
From Down and Here to Up and There.
Stars and sky, sky and stars
Make us feel the prison bars.

Suppose it done. Now we ride
Closed in steel, up there, outside;
Through our port-holes see the vast
Heaven-scape go rushing past.
Shall we? All that meets the eye
Is sky and stars, stars and sky.

Points of light with black between
Hang like a painted scene
Motionless, no nearer there

Than on Earth, everywhere
Equidistant from our ship.
Heaven has given us the slip.

Hush, be still. Outer space
Is a concept, not a place.
Try no more. Where we are
Never can be sky or star.
From prison, in a prison, we fly;
There's no way into the sky.

C. S. LEWIS

Explanation

When the pillars of smoke, that towered between
    heaven and earth
On the day we died, have thinned in the wind and
    drifted
And the hooded crow flaps home across the volcanic
    sky,
Somewhere beyond and below the littered horizon
(Out of the cave into the cold air)
Man, I suppose, will emerge and grow wise and read
What we have written in guilt, again with an innocent
    eye.

Then, if the desperate song we sang like storm-cocks
At the first flash, survives the ultimate thunder
To be dreamily misunderstood by the children of
    quieter men,
Remember that we who lived in the creeping shadow
(Dark over woodland, cloud and water)
Looked upon beauty often as though for the last time
And loved all things the more, that might never be
    seen again;

Who chewed the leaf, uncertain of seeing the haw-
    thorn
Scatter its stars the length of a lane in summer,
Or fingered the sparrow's egg that might never be
    born a bird;
And wondered, even, whether the windflaw moving
Silently over the water's surface
Should gain the distant edge of the lake in safety
Before the inferno struck, whose echoes shall never
    be heard.

I sing to a child unborn, begotten in guilt
By us who have made the world unfit for his coming.
Our only comfort: that Christ was born in the cold.
I know, I know that a legion of singers before us
Looked their last on much that was lovely
And perished as we must perish. But who will
    remember
That most of them wept and died only because they
    were old?

                        PAUL DEHN

Bedtime Story

Long long ago when the world was a wild place
Planted with bushes and peopled by apes, our
Mission Brigade was at work in the jungle.
   Hard by the Congo

Once, when a foraging detail was active
Scouting for green-fly, it came on a grey man, the
Last living man, in the branch of a baobab
   Stalking a monkey.

Earlier men had disposed of, for pleasure,
Creatures whose names we scarcely remember—
Zebra, rhinoceros, elephants, wart-hog,
    Lion, rats, deer. But

After the wars had extinguished the cities
Only the wild ones were left, half-naked
Near the Equator: and here was the last one,
    Starved for a monkey.

By then the Mission Brigade had encountered
Hundreds of such men: and their procedure,
History tells us, was only to feed them:
    Find them and feed them;

Those were the orders. And this was the last one.
Nobody knew that he was, but he was. Mud
Caked on his flat grey flanks. He was crouched, half-
    armed with a shaved spear

Glinting beneath broad leaves. When their jaws cut
Swathes through the bark and he saw fine teeth
    shine,
Round eyes roll round and forked arms waver
    Huge as the rough trunks

Over his head, he was frightened. Our workers
Marched through the Congo before he was born, but
This was the first time perhaps that he'd seen one.
    Staring in hot still

Silence, he crouched there: then jumped. With a
    long swing
Down from his branch, he had angled his spear too
Quickly, before they could hold him, and hurled it
    Hard at the soldier

Leading the detail. How could he know Queen's
Orders were only to help him? The soldier
Winced when the tipped spear pricked him. Un-
    sheathing his
    Sting was a reflex.

Later the Queen was informed. There were no more
Men. An impetuous soldier had killed off,
Purely by chance, the penultimate primate.
    When she was certain,

Squadrons of workers were fanned through the Congo
Detailed to bring back the man's picked bones to be
Sealed in the archives in amber. I'm quite sure
    Nobody found them

After the most industrious search, though.
Where had the bones gone? Over the earth, dear,
Ground by the teeth of the termites, blown by the
    Wind, like the dodo's.

                                    GEORGE MacBETH

Your Attention Please

The Polar DEW has just warned that
A nuclear rocket strike of
At least one thousand megatons
Has been launched by the enemy
Directly at our major cities.
This announcement will take
Two and a quarter minutes to make,
You therefore have a further
Eight and a quarter minutes
To comply with the shelter

Requirements published in the Civil
Defence Code—section Atomic Attack.
A specially shortened Mass
Will be broadcast at the end
Of this announcement—
Protestant and Jewish services
Will begin simultaneously—
Select your wave length immediately
According to instructions
In the Defence Code. Do not
Take well-loved pets (including birds)
Into your shelter—they will consume
Fresh air. Leave the old and bed-
ridden, you can do nothing for them.
Remember to press the sealing
Switch when everyone is in
The shelter. Set the radiation
Aerial, turn on the geiger barometer.
Turn off your Television now.
Turn off your radio immediately
The Services end. At the same time
Secure explosion plugs in the ears
Of each member of your family. Take
Down your plasma flasks. Give your children
The pills marked one and two
In the C.D. green container, then put
Them to bed. Do not break
The inside airlock seals until
The radiation All Clear shows
(Watch for the cuckoo in your
perspex panel), or your District
Touring Doctor rings your bell.
If before this, your air becomes
Exhausted or if any of your family
Is critically injured, administer
The capsules marked 'Valley Forge'

(Red Pocket in No. 1 Survival Kit)
For painless death. (Catholics
Will have been instructed by their priests
What to do in this eventuality.)
This announcement is ending. Our President
Has already given orders for
Massive retaliation—it will be
Decisive. Some of us may die.
Remember, statistically
It is not likely to be you.
All flags are flying fully dressed
On Government buildings   the sun is shining.
Death is the least we have to fear.
We are all in the hands of God,
Whatever happens happens by His Will.
Now go quickly to your shelters.

PETER PORTER

The Horses

Barely a twelvemonth after
The seven days war that put the world to sleep,
Late in the evening the strange horses came.
By then we had made our covenant with silence,
But in the first few days it was so still
We listened to our breathing and were afraid.
On the second day
The radios failed; we turned the knobs; no answer.
On the third day a warship passed us, heading north,
Dead bodies piled on the deck. On the sixth day
A plane plunged over us into the sea. Thereafter
Nothing. The radios dumb;
And still they stand in corners of our kitchens,
And stand, perhaps, turned on, in a million rooms
All over the world. But now if they should speak,

If on a sudden they should speak again,
If on the stroke of noon a voice should speak,
We would not listen, we would not let it bring
That bad old world that swallowed its children quick
At one great gulp. We would not have it again.
Sometimes we think of the nations lying asleep,
Curled blindly in impenetrable sorrow,
And then the thought confounds us with its strange-
      ness.

The tractors lie about our fields; at evening
They look like dank sea-monsters couched and
      waiting.
We leave them where they are and let them rust:
'They'll moulder away and be like other loam.'
We make our oxen drag our rusty ploughs,
Long laid aside. We have gone back
Far past our fathers' land.
                              And then, that evening
Late in the summer the strange horses came.
We heard a distant tapping on the road,
A deepening drumming; it stopped, went on again
And at the corner changed to hollow thunder.
We saw the heads
Like a wild wave charging and were afraid.
We had sold our horses in our fathers' time
To buy new tractors. Now they were strange to us
As fabulous steeds set on an ancient shield
Or illustrations in a book of knights.
We did not dare go near them. Yet they waited,
Stubborn and shy, as if they had been sent
By an old command to find our whereabouts
And that long-lost archaic companionship.
In the first moment we had never a thought
That they were creatures to be owned and used.
Among them were some half-a-dozen colts

Dropped in some wilderness of the broken world,
Yet new as if they had come from their own Eden.
Since then they have pulled our ploughs and borne
   our loads,
But that free servitude still can pierce our hearts.
Our life is changed; their coming our beginning.

EDWIN MUIR

ACKNOWLEDGMENTS

Thanks are due to the following for kind permission to print the poems included in this Anthology:

Dannie Abse and Messrs Hutchinson and Co. (Publishers), Ltd, for poems from *Tenants of This House*; W. H. Auden and Messrs Faber and Faber, Ltd, for poem from *Collected Shorter Poems*; George Barker and Messrs Faber and Faber, Ltd, for poem from *Collected Poems, 1930–1955*; Francis Berry and Messrs Routledge and Kegan Paul, Ltd, for poems from *The Morant Bay* and *Ghosts of Greenland*; John Betjeman and Messrs John Murray, Ltd, for poems from *Collected Poems* and *High and Low*; Edmund Blunden and Messrs A. D. Peters and Co., for poem; Edwin Brock and the Scorpion Press, for poems from *With Love from Judas*; Alan Brownjohn and the Digby Press, for poem from *The Railings*; Charles Causley and Messrs Rupert Hart-Davis, Ltd, for poems from *Union Street* and *Johnny Alleluia*; Peter Champkin for poem from *For the Employed*, and Messrs Robert Hale, Ltd, for poem from *The Enmity of Noon*; Richard Church and Messrs William Heinemann, Ltd, for poems from *The Inheritors*, and Laurence Pollinger, Ltd, and the Editor of *The Listener* for 'Street Accident'; Leonard Clark, for poems: Tony Connor and the Oxford University Press, for poem from *The Lodgers*; Hilary Corke and Messrs Martin Secker and Warburg, Ltd, for poems from *The Early Drowned*; Iain Crichton Smith and Messrs Eyre and Spottiswoode, Ltd, for poem from *The Law and the Grace*; Paul Dehn and Messrs Hamish Hamilton, Ltd, for poems from *Fern on the Rock*; Patric Dickinson, for 'The Dam' from *Stone in the Midst*, and Messrs Chatto and Windus, Ltd, for poems from *The World I See* and *This Cold Universe*; Ronald Duncan and David Higham Associates, Ltd, for poem from *The Solitudes*; Clifford Dyment, for 'Someone Looking', and Messrs J. M. Dent and Sons, Ltd, for poem from *Experiences and Places*; Nissim Ezekiel and Messrs Hutchinson and Co. (Publishers), Ltd, for poem from *New Poems, '65*; the Executors of Robert Frost, Messrs Jonathan Cape, Ltd, and Messrs

Holt, Rinehart and Winston, Inc., for poem from *The Complete Poems of Robert Frost*; John Fuller and Messrs Chatto and Windus, Ltd, for poems from *Fairground Music* and *The Tree that Walked*; Roy Fuller and Messrs Andre Deutsch, Ltd, for poem from *Collected Poems*; Robert Graves and Messrs Cassell and Co., Ltd, for poems from *Collected Poems, 1965*; the Executors of Sir George Rostrevor Hamilton and Messrs William Heinemann, Ltd, for poem from *Collected Poems and Epigrams*; Seamus Heaney and Messrs Faber and Faber, Ltd, for poems from *Death of a Naturalist*, and the Editor of *The Listener*, for 'Rookery'; John Heath-Stubbs and Messrs Routledge and Kegan Paul, Ltd, for poems from *The Blue Fly in his Heart* and *Selected Poems*; Phoebe Hesketh and Messrs Rupert Hart-Davis, Ltd, for poem from *Prayer for Sun*; Philip Hobsbaum, for poem; Ted Hughes and Messrs Faber and Faber, Ltd, for poems from *Lupercal* and *The Hawk in the Rain*; Elizabeth Jennings for 'The Smell of Cooking', and Messrs Andre Deutsch, Ltd, for poems from *A Way of Looking, Song for a Birth or a Death*, and *A Sense of the World*; Mrs Agnes Johnson, for poem by the late Geoffrey Johnson; Jenny Joseph and the Scorpion Press, for poem from *The Unlooked-for Season*, and Messrs Hutchinson and Co. (Publishers), Ltd, and the Editor of *The Listener*, for poem from *New Poems, '65*; James Kirkup and the Oxford University Press, for poems from *The Prodigal Son*; Philip Larkin and Messrs Faber and Faber, Ltd, for poem from *The Whitsun Weddings*; Laurence Lerner and Messrs Chatto and Windus, Ltd, for poem from *The Directions of Memory*; the Executors of C. S. Lewis and Messrs Geoffrey Bles, Ltd, for poems from *The Collected Poems of C. S. Lewis*; Edward Lucie-Smith and the Oxford University Press, for poem from *A Tropical Childhood*; George MacBeth and the Scorpion Press, for poem from *The Broken Places*; Norman MacCaig and Messrs Chatto and Windus, Ltd, for poems from *A Common Grace, Surroundings* and *Measures*, and the Editor of *The Times Literary Supplement*, for 'Sleeping Compartment'; the Executors of Louis Mac-Neice and Messrs Faber and Faber, Ltd, for poems from *Collected Poems* and *The Burning Perch*; Edwin V. Milner and the Editor of *The Listener*, for poem; the Executors of Edwin Muir and Messrs Faber and Faber, Ltd, for poems from *Collected Poems*; Richard Murphy and Messrs Faber and Faber, Ltd, for poem from *Sailing to an Island*; Norman Nicholson, for poem; Ruth Pitter and the Cresset Press, for poem from *Still by Choice*; Peter Porter and the Scorpion Press, for poem from *Once Bitten, Twice Shy*; John Pudney and Messrs Putnam, Ltd, for poem from *Collected Poems*; Peter Redgrove and Messrs Routledge and Kegan Paul, Ltd, for poem from *The Force*; Henry Reed and the Editor of *The Listener* for poem; the Executors of Bernard Spencer and Messrs Alan Ross, for poems from *Collected Poems*; Hubert Nicholson and Messrs William Heinemann, Ltd, for poems from *Voices in a Giant City* by the late A. S. J. Tessimond; R. S. Thomas and Messrs Rupert Hart-Davis, Ltd, for poems from *Song at the Year's Turning* and *The Bread of Truth*; Anthony Thwaite and the Oxford University Press, for poems from *The Owl in the Trees* and *The Stones of Emptiness*; the Executors of Vernon Watkins and Messrs Faber and Faber, Ltd, for poem from *Cypress and Acacia*; Bernard Gilhooly for 'At 30,000 Feet'.

It is much regretted that, in spite of every effort, the Editor has been unable to trace the copyright holders of the following: 'Anthology' by Robert Gittings; 'Death' by K. W. Gransden; 'Telephone Conversation' by Wole Soyinka; 'In Memory of My Grandfather' by Edward Storey; and 'Loneliness' by Margaret Taylor.

INDEX OF FIRST LINES